Industrial Organization

Cintya Lanchimba

Industrial Organization

The Economics of Markets, Firms, and Competition

palgrave
macmillan

Cintya Lanchimba
Departamento de Economía
Cuantitativa
Escuela Politécnica Nacional
QUITO, Ecuador

ISBN 978-3-032-10905-7 ISBN 978-3-032-10906-4 (eBook)
https://doi.org/10.1007/978-3-032-10906-4

Cover Credit: @Alex Linch shutterstock.com

This Palgrave Macmillan imprint is published by the registered company Springer Nature Switzerland AG
The registered company address is: Gewerbestrasse 11, 6330 Cham, Switzerland

To my husband, Juan Pablo Díaz, to my family and friends, and to my mentor and friend, Professor Muriel Fadairo—with gratitude for their love, encouragement, and inspiration along this journey.

Preface

This book focuses on the study of Industrial Economics and is aimed at first- and second-cycle university students. Its purpose is to serve as a tool to improve the understanding of interactions within and between firms. Therefore, the fundamental objective is to analyze firms and markets as they exist in the real world.

The introduction of the book begins with a review of the history of Industrial Economics. From there, the simplest market structure known in microeconomics is examined: perfect competition. This starting point allows for a clear frame of reference to be established, by understanding what economists consider to be an ideal market structure. With this idealized model in mind, market structures that deviate from perfect competition are explored. The perfect competition model highlights the importance of this competitive ideal, in which consumers retain most or all of their surplus, and serves as a basis for comparison with imperfect competition models, those that do not meet one or more of the assumptions of the perfect competition model.

The second part of the book describes several models of imperfect competition: (i) monopoly, where a single producer dominates the market, which gives it some power when setting prices; (ii) oligopoly, characterized by the presence of a few suppliers that possess market power similar to that of a monopoly; and (iii) monopolistic competition, among others.

In the third part, market regulations and competition policies are examined. The historical origin of competition laws and tools for measuring market power are presented.

Finally, information economics is introduced, focusing on Contract Theory. This final section focuses on the principal-agent model within the context of information economics, highlighting how asymmetric information and incentives can influence economic decision-making.

QUITO, Ecuador Cintya Lanchimba

Acknowledgments

I want to begin by expressing my sincere gratitude to the Departamento de Economía Cuantitativa at the Escuela Politécnica Nacional, whose academic environment and support have been instrumental in the development of this book.

I also want to express my love and gratitude to my family. To my father Enrique and my mother Fanny, for their unconditional love. To my siblings Alex, Tania, and Gricelda, for their constant presence and sincere affection. To my nephews Aldo and Gabriel, whose spontaneity, tenderness, and joy brighten every step of the journey. And to Toribio, my loyal four-legged companion, for his quiet presence and unconditional affection.

My heartfelt thanks go to my husband, Juan Pablo Díaz, for walking by my side with love, patience, and trust. I also warmly thank my family-in-law for their sincere affection, especially my parents-in-law, Marcos and Jackeline.

I am sincerely grateful to my friends for their invaluable contributions: to Ramiro Torres and Miguel Yangari, for his assistance in revising the LaTeX manuscript; to Andrea Bonilla, for reviewing the content to ensure coherence and clarity; to Sara Ortiz and Julio Medina, for their style revisions; and to Yasmín Salazar, Paulina Salazar, and José Ramírez, for their unwavering moral support and encouragement.

A very special acknowledgment goes to Diego Albuja, whose careful English coherence and linguistic revision of the manuscript greatly improved its clarity and overall quality.

I also extend my deepest appreciation to the anonymous reviewers, whose constructive feedback contributed to improving this work, and to the editorial team at Springer, for their support throughout the publication process.

Finally, to all those who, directly or indirectly, have supported me, believed in me, and contributed to the completion of this project—my deepest thanks.

Contents

List of Figures

List of Tables

CHAPTER 1

Introduction

Industrial Economics or Industrial Organization, the latter name known from Jean Tirole's book,[1] is the discipline that studies the organization of companies and markets in the real world. Thus, it constitutes the theoretical framework for understanding firm strategies and market mechanisms.

We will consider Industrial Economics as an extension of microeconomics. This implies that we will continue to maintain the principle of the rationality of agents. This assumption establishes that there is a form of exchange between the agents and the market is the mechanism that guarantees the efficient allocation of resources. In other words, two conditions are needed:

Condition 1 (exchange): Consumers and producers exchange on the market, where price is the resource allocation mechanism. Economic agents act voluntarily, that is, no one forces them to accept an exchange.

Condition 2 (market): The market includes all those goods with a degree of substitutability between them. Furthermore, this degree of substitutability must be high enough to make the adopted definition useful for the proposed analysis.

[1] Jean Tirole was awarded the Nobel Prize in Economics in 2014 for his work on Industrial Economics.

C. Lanchimba, *Industrial Organization*,
https://doi.org/10.1007/978-3-032-10906-4_1

Industrial Economics focuses on the organization of markets and companies. Not only does this discipline deal with industry, but it also analyzes services and trade. Particularly, it focuses on (i) how a firm can generate a competitive advantage or obtain market power and (ii) how it can improve or keep that power. The answers to these questions are of interest not only to business decision-makers (in marketing and strategies) but also to policymakers.

Thus, market power refers to a firm's ability to achieve high sales margins, that is, to sell at a price above marginal cost. According to Professor Thierry Pernard (2014),[2] market power is linked first to the market structure, which can be understood by the degree of concentration of supply, product differentiation, and barriers to entry.

A firm can also increase its market power and the level of competitiveness by implementing appropriate strategies that would engage in changing market structures. This is the case of strategies to increase barriers to entry or the degree of market concentration. Some of these strategies may be considered illegal and subject to sanctions by antitrust laws.

In other words, Industrial Economics focuses on the functioning of markets and how companies compete in these markets. This is also the main interest of microeconomics, but Industrial Economics focuses on imperfect competition, which encompasses the spectrum between the utopian vision of pure and perfect competition and the counterexample of monopoly. It also takes into account strategies such as advertising, product differentiation, and investments in research and development, among others.

In this context, it is pertinent to ask about the use of Industrial Organization. Industrial Economics provides a technical basis for market regulatory policy (competition policy, sector regulations), industrial policy, innovation policy, and regional planning. Therefore, Industrial Economics provides conceptual analysis tools to analyze markets and evaluate and anticipate corporate strategies. Therefore, it is intended for both entrepreneurs and market regulatory agents. When studying companies, it focuses on business consultants and strategies that analyze the market to anticipate the behavior of companies. On the regulators' side, it is addressed to the regulatory authorities, generally to the competition authorities involved in avoiding the negative consequences that may arise

[2] Professor at the University of Rennes, France; expert in Industrial Organization.

from market power concentration. For example, Ecuador has established the Superintendency of Companies and the Superintendency of Control of Market Power. Likewise, at the end of the twentieth century, the "antitrust" law (see Chap. 6) appeared in the United States (Sherman Act of 1890). This law was approved to protect competition, particularly, in the fight against cartels.

Thus, this book will review several of the most relevant theories related to this topic and provide the reader with basic elements to understand how companies behave in imperfect markets.

1.1 Historical Milestones in the Study of Industrial Organization

The study of Industrial Organization, or the functioning of markets, began to develop systematically in the 1930s and was consolidated after the Second World War, with the appearance of the structuralist school, also known as the Harvard school. This school of thought, led by emblematic figures such as Joe Bain and Edward Mason, laid the foundations for the analysis of market structures and their relationship with economic performance (Bain 1959; Mason 1939).

However, it is important to note that theoretical market models did not emerge exclusively at this stage. There are previous contributions that have been fundamental to understanding market dynamics, including oligopoly models. A prominent example is the work of Antoine Augustin Cournot, who in *Recherches sur les principes mathématiques de la théorie des richesses* (1838) developed a pioneering model of competition between firms in markets with few participants. His analysis of the strategic decisions of firms regarding the quantities produced and the impact of these on prices constitutes one of the first formal approaches to the study of oligopolies (Cournot 1838).

Despite the relevance of these previous contributions, in this part of the book, we will focus on the main schools of thought that emerged in the twentieth century, with a special emphasis on the Harvard structuralist school and other related currents. Oligopolies, due to their complexity and importance in the modern market structure, have a space reserved in this book in the Chap. 4, where we will explore their characteristics, theoretical models, and practical applications in greater depth.

1.1.1 *Harvard School*

Early developments in Industrial Economics have their origin in the so-called Harvard school. This school was developed between the years 1930 and 1960 to try to provide guidelines for competition policy.

The works of Robinson (1934) and Chamberlin (1933) focus on the theory of imperfect competition. This school was developed as an attempt to give guidelines to competition policy, through empirical studies, to determine whether the conduct of a firm was illegal, based on certain characteristics of the firm (e.g., the size of the firm).

Later in 1939, Mason established the Structure-Conduct-Performance (SCP) paradigm, which is central to the Industrial Economy because it argues that the presence of competing companies influences companies. Thus, the *market structure* of the market (number of sellers, differentiation, costs, etc.) exerts an influence, directly and indirectly through behavior (price, investments, etc.), on the *market performance* of the market (efficiency, variety of products, etc.). Certain market structures (monopoly, oligopoly) lead to socially suboptimal situations (the surplus obtained by firms reduces the consumers' utility). Regulatory policies (free competition policies) can be used to change the market structure, which is why they are part of the theoretical foundations of competition policy. The reactions of current or potential competing companies are considered, depending on the existence of barriers to entry, product differentiation strategies, and the behavior of these companies.

Therefore, our emphasis is placed on the need to analyze noncompetitive behavior of market structures. Creating a classification of market structures is proposed. Moreover, the fundamental part of the analysis is to explain the firms' behavior through a review of these market structures.

In 1968, Bain further developed the SCP paradigm (standard approach to study Industrial Organization) which breaks down the market into three elements: (i) market structure, (ii) behavior of market participants, and (iii) market performance. This structuralist approach proposes that market structure is the number of sellers on the market; the degree of product differentiation, the cost structure, the degree of vertical integration of sellers, entry conditions, and firm size, among others, determine the firms' behavior. This behavior is considered in terms of price, research and development, and advertising research, among others. This behavior leads to market performance, which refers to efficiency, the price-to-marginal-cost ratio, product variety, innovation rate, utility, and distribution (J. Tirole

1988). On the other hand, demand (elasticity of demand), technology (economies of scale), and regulation are determined exogenously.

Specifically, to study the S-C-R paradigm, econometric regressions were carried out between the structure, the conduct, the results, and some exogenous variables to find some regularities of the market. In this context, Tirole (1988) points out that the limits of the paradigm are as follows: (i) they used an empirical, descriptive, static approach, (ii) the demonstration of the results was carried out through stylized facts, and (iii) the comparison of the exogenous variables between the different sectors, downplaying the importance of the data.

1.1.2 Chicago School

Later advances were made in 1970 with the so-called Chicago school. The main exponents of this school are George Stigler and Aaron Director. Here, the causality between the elements of the previous triptych is reversed, that is, *Behavior* → *Performance* → *Structure*. The market structure is no longer the explanatory variable but becomes the explained part. It is then a benevolent view of market behavior, in which the market regulatory mechanism is free competition between companies. This perspective is based on the premise that market forces tend toward natural efficiency, provided that regulatory barriers are minimal and there is no significant interference from the state (Demsetz 1968; Stigler 1971).

However, the Chicago school lacks tools to describe strategic interactions, i.e., they do not explain behaviors empirically. This is because their approach is more focused on general theories of market behavior than on the detailed analysis of specific strategic dynamics between firms, which has led to criticism from other schools, such as the neostructuralist school, which consider these interactions key to understanding phenomena such as oligopolies and monopolies.

The founding fathers of this school are Baumol et al. (1982). The elements of the triptych are the potential structure of the market, behavior, and performance. The emphasis is on the role of potential participants in a market. The theory suggests that, even in markets with a small number of firms, the threat of entry of new competitors can discipline existing firms, encouraging competitive behaviors similar to those in a perfectly competitive market (Baumol et al. 1982).

We then speak of the theory of contestable markets, according to which a market is contestable depending on the level of entry barriers. Contestable means competition despite the small number of firms. A market is considered contestable if the costs of entry and exit are low enough to allow the immediate entry of new participants in response to noncompetitive behavior, limiting the power of established firms (Shepherd 1984).

For the defenders of the Chicago school, the competitive model is quite adequate to explain everything that happens in markets. In this view, regulatory interventions are often seen as unnecessary or even harmful, since they interfere with the natural mechanisms of the market to correct inefficiencies. This does not mean that the monopoly does not exist, but that it is only temporary and disappears with the entry of new firms. Therefore, the possibilities of strategic behavior are limited. In addition, most enduring monopolies are creations of the state. According to this school, the role of the state should be limited to guaranteeing freedom of entry and exit in markets and protecting property rights, leaving market dynamics to determine the final structure (Posner 1975).

1.1.3 The New Industrial Economy

The New Industrial Economics, also known as post-Chicago, emerged around 1980 as a significant evolution in the analysis of markets and firms. It focuses on strategic interactions between economic agents, using noncooperative game theory as its central tool, marking a departure from previous, more simplistic, and deterministic approaches. This approach formally introduces rigorous mathematical models and uses advanced statistical and econometric tools, allowing for a more detailed empirical analysis of actual markets.

Game theory becomes the reference tool of the new industrial economists, providing a theoretical framework for modeling the strategic behavior of agents and interactions between firms in imperfect markets or with incomplete information (see Appendix 8.1). These models incorporate asymmetric information, a key concept that describes situations in which one or both parties lack complete information about the actions or characteristics of the other.[3]

[3] One or both parties do not have complete information about what the other does.

On the other hand, econometric techniques have allowed industrial economists to empirically examine the relationship between market structures, firm behavior, and economic performance, thus strengthening the validation of theoretical models. In this context, the theory of Industrial Organization, named after the influential book by Jean Tirole (1988), constitutes the core of this new Industrial Economics. Tirole's approach combines theoretical analysis with empirical validation, establishing a bridge between theory and economic reality.

The New Industrial Economics also presents a renewed strategic perspective on the SCP (Structure-Conduct-Performance) paradigm, because it places special emphasis on how firms' strategies shape market structures and vice versa. The central idea is that structure, behavior, and performance interact bidirectionally, breaking with the unidirectional view of previous approaches. This change means that firms' strategic behavior not only responds to market structures but also actively modifies them through decisions such as pricing, mergers, product differentiation, and entry or exit strategies.

Consequently, a market structure depends on strategies adopted by firms. For example, a merger strategy can lead to a greater concentration of supply in a market, significantly altering the structure of this market. Unlike the Chicago School, New Industrial Economics argues that firms can significantly influence market outcomes, not only in terms of price but also in terms of quantity, quality, and variety of products offered.

Empirically, the New Industrial Economics studies a wide variety of market phenomena, including economic concentration, product differentiation, cost structure, competitive behavior, barriers to entry, and market power dynamics. This research has found specific applications in sectors such as telecommunications, energy, and digital technologies, where markets have unique characteristics that require tailored models.

In short, the New Industrial Economics almost abandons the notion of perfect competition, considering it an unrealistic and limited description of actual markets. Instead, it focuses on analyzing the strategic behaviors of agents, the information asymmetries, and the complex dynamics that characterize contemporary markets. This has led to a significant advance in our understanding of how firms operate and compete in real markets, providing academics and regulators with a solid basis for economic analysis and policy-making.

Finally, since the 2000s, the New Industrial Economics has increasingly focused on applying specific models to key sectors, such as telecommunications, energy, and digital technologies. Moreover, the adoption of innovative methodological tools, such as empirical Industrial Organization, experimental economics, and behavioral economics, has allowed it to enrich and diversify its analytical approach, adapting it to the challenges of the modern world.

1.2 Competitive Behavior

1.2.1 Introduction

In this section, we will analyze perfect competition as an ideal model of standard microeconomics. We introduce this model because it can be used to evaluate other forms of competition. A market is in a situation of perfect competition if the agents involved in this market (buyers or sellers) have a competitive behavior.

An economic agent (buyer or seller) has a competitive behavior if he considers (with or without certainty) that the market price is given and that the actions he can carry out will not change this price. In other words, competitive behavior implies that the agents believe they do not have market power. Not only does this absence of market power guarantee that prices reflect the conditions of supply and demand, but it also ensures that resources are allocated efficiently, maximizing social welfare (Varian 2015). This hypothesis of competitive behavior is independent of the number of agents in the market; what matters is that the agents believe in the absence of a price change, that is, they are "price takers."

Naturally, it is easier to rationalize such expectations when the number of agents is high. Therefore, regardless of the number of agents in the market, it is possible to calculate a competitive equilibrium when they behave competitively. This condition means that any deviation from the equilibrium price will result in automatic forces that adjust it again, ensuring market stability (Mas-Colell et al. 1995).

In perfect competition, prices make the plans of the agents involved compatible, that is, all participants in that market are satisfied. On the one hand, producers buy quantities of goods, which we call factors of production, and combine them to obtain one or more products. For example, consumers buy the goods produced by producers. They own the production factors and get their income by supplying them to producers. In addition, there is no economic agent in charge of setting prices. However, we sometimes resort to the fictitious figure of the auctioneer, who proposes raising prices in markets with excess demand and lowering them where there is excess supply until reaching equilibrium prices at which exchanges occur. The reason is that transactions take place at prices that meet certain conditions and that prices are not modified by observations made in the market.

Likewise, market prices cause the market to empty since consumers and producers are satisfied with their consumption and production decisions, respectively. In this context, equilibrium is a desirable and efficient state, since any deviation would result in a loss of efficiency in the distribution of resources (Arrow and Debreu 1954).

To understand perfect competition, the fundamental hypotheses of this basic model are presented below, which come from standard microeconomics:

Atomicity deals with multiple buyers and producers that prevent a particular influence on the price. Therefore, the agents are price takers or price acceptors. Atomicity is essential to prevent the formation of monopolies or oligopolies that distort the market (Pindyck and Rubinfeld 2009).

Fluidity assumes that any agent, buyer, or producer can enter the market at any time. This principle guarantees that the barriers to entry and exit are zero, promoting competition and avoiding monopolistic rents (Carlton and Perloff 2008).

These first two hypotheses guarantee a pure market far from any monopolistic structure.

Homogeneity It is assumed that the goods produced are strictly identical and perfectly substitutable. Therefore, the consumer will focus exclusively on the price of the good to make his choice. This homogeneity eliminates consumer's subjective preferences, leaving the price as the only determinant of demand (Stiglitz 1987).

Mobility States that the production factors, labor, and capital can move freely. Resource mobility ensures that companies can adapt to changes in demand, minimizing waste and promoting efficiency (Friedman and Miles 2002).

Transparency Economic agents have perfect information, that is, total and free. In other words, there is information symmetry. Transparency eliminates information asymmetries that can lead to inefficient markets or even market failure (Ackerlof 1970).

Not only does the combination of these five assumptions define a perfectly competitive market, but it also provides an ideal framework for assessing actual deviations from modern markets and their relative efficiency (Samuelson and Nordhaus 2010).

On the other hand, Industrial Economics enunciates seven postulates, which are similar and complementary to the hypotheses of pure and perfect competition:

The Product Is Homogeneous Consumers are indifferent to the origin of the product.

Symmetric information instead Consumers Are Indifferent to the Origin of the Product There is perfect information or, in other words, "market transparency." Agents who participate in the market have complete (relevant) information on the price and quality of the product.

The Price Is Determined by the Market An atomized market illustrates this scenario. Buyers and sellers cannot individually influence the market price, which implies they are "price takers" or "price acceptors" since they consider the price as given.

Transaction Costs Are Zero There are no costs or entry fees to access the market. This scenario implies that administrative or economic barriers do not affect agents' decisions (Coase 1937).

There Is No Externality Each firm assumes the total cost of its production.

There Is Freedom of Entry and Exit for Companies Or, in other words, market fluidity. Companies can enter or leave the market at any time without having to incur special costs. In other words, there are no barriers to entry or exit. This freedom promotes innovation and ensures that only the most efficient firms survive in the market (Schumpeter 1942).

Perfect Divisibility of Production Firms can produce and consumers can buy any product on the market.

These postulates complement the framework of perfect competition, underlining the importance of ideal conditions for the efficient functioning of markets (Tirole 1988).

The existence of supply and demand constitutes the core of any economic system. A consumer's demand depends not only on tangible factors such as income, the price of the desired good, and other goods' prices but also on intangible elements such as preferences, future expectations, and personal circumstances. In the case of normal goods, it is common to observe that when the price of a good, such as food, decreases, its demand increases or when income increases, consumption does too. However, some goods contradict this trend such as inferior goods. For example, Lanchimba and Diaz (2017) provide evidence that in Ecuador, as people's income increases, their desire to have children decreases, suggesting that children are considered inferior goods, an idea aligned with the approaches of Baker (1960).

This behavior of goods is reflected in movements along the demand curve, influenced by external factors such as price variations or changes in income. It is important to note that these movements respond not only to direct changes but also to interactions between complementary and substitute goods. For example, fuel price reduction could increase the demand for vehicles, while an increase in public transport prices could have a similar effect.

As for supply, its behavior in the market is intrinsically linked to the elasticity of goods. Elasticity, as a measure of sensitivity to changes in price, plays a crucial role in the decision-making of producers and consumers.

$$\epsilon = \frac{\frac{\Delta q}{q}}{\frac{\Delta p}{p}} = \frac{\delta q}{\delta p}\frac{p}{q} \tag{1.2.1}$$

The elasticity of demand (1.2.1) is measured as the quotient between the price p and the quantity q multiplied by the derivative of demand with respect to the price (slope of demand). If demand is elastic ($\epsilon > 1$), small changes in price lead to significant variations in the quantity demanded, as is the case with luxury goods or nonessential products. In contrast, inelastic demand ($\epsilon < 1$) is observed for indispensable products, such as certain medicines, where even substantial price changes do not significantly affect the quantity demanded. This sensitivity influences not only prices but also production strategies and tax policies designed to minimize social losses.

1.2.2 *Profit Maximization*

Profit maximization is the cornerstone of any business, leading the producer to solve an optimization problem where he seeks to balance costs and income. Equation (1.2.2), which defines profit $\pi(q)$ as the difference between total revenue and total cost of production, encapsulates this basic principle, but, in practice, firms face additional constraints, such as capacity limitations, competition, and regulation.

$$\pi(q) = pq - C(q) \tag{1.2.2}$$

where p is the price, q is the quantity produced, and $C(q)$ is the total cost of production.

Because this is a price-taking firm, *quantity* is its only variable to maximize profit:

$$\frac{\delta\pi}{\delta q} = MR - MC \Rightarrow MR = MC \tag{1.2.3}$$

The firm makes a profit as long as the revenue from the sale of an additional unit is greater than the cost of production, that is, when the marginal revenue MR is greater than the marginal cost MC ($MR > MC$).[4] However, in equilibrium, Eq. (1.2.2) shows that $MR = MC = p$. Therefore, for a competitive firm, the optimal production rule is to increase production until marginal cost MC equals price. Likewise, the producer's profits are equal to zero.[5] In other words, for a price-taking firm, where the only decision variable is the quantity produced, the maximization rule dictates that production should continue until marginal revenue equals marginal cost ($MR = MC = p$).

It is interesting to note that, under perfect competition, economic profits tend to zero in the long term. This does not imply that firms

[4] Marginal cost is the cost of producing an additional unit, while marginal revenue is the revenue from the sale of an additional unit.

[5] Equation (1.2.2) can be rewritten as $\pi = pq - MCq$ by replacing the maximization rule $MR = MC = p$; we observe that $\pi = 0$.

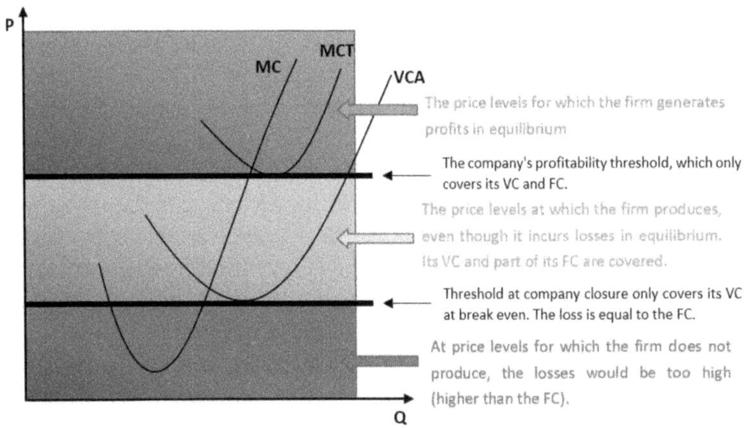

Fig. 1.1 Closing thresholds. Source: Author

are unprofitable but that economic profits, which include the opportunity cost of resources, equal the normal profits that motivate permanence in the market. This equilibrium guarantees that resources are used efficiently, maximizing social welfare.

Therefore, a firm only produces if it is profitable, that is, if its revenue is higher than its recoverable costs. Recoverable costs are variable costs, while sunk costs are fixed costs. Therefore, revenue must be at least as high as variable costs (see Fig. 1.1). This is precisely what is known as the *closing threshold of the firm*, where the price is equal to the average variable cost (AVC)[6] and the marginal cost ($MC = \frac{\delta C}{\delta q}$).

When $AVC < p < MC$, the firm loses money if we consider all costs and revenues, but it can minimize its losses. It is better to produce and recover the surplus of income over variable costs than to close and have no income because producing allows partially offsetting sunk costs.[7] Thus,

[6] The production cost is the sum of the fixed cost, which is independent of the production volume and the variable cost, which depends on the production volume $C = FC + VC$. Likewise, the unit costs of goods can be analyzed using the average cost by dividing the total cost by the number of units produced ($AC = \frac{C}{q}$) or the average variable cost ($AVC = \frac{AC}{q}$).

[7] Sunk costs are all those costs that the producer has incurred in the past and that cannot be recovered.

when fixed costs are sunk, the firm produces $p > AVC$, and firm does not produce otherwise. This range, where $p < AVC$, is known as the "stoppage threshold."

On the other hand, the part of MC located above the stoppage threshold, i.e., where it intersects the AVC, is the firm's supply curve. The profit per unit corresponds to the difference between the price and the average total cost. The firm's short-term supply curve is the rising part of the marginal cost curve located above the average variable cost curve (see Fig. 1.1). In the long term, this dynamic is amplified by the entry and exit of firms from the market, leading to a stabilization of the break-even point and the establishment of an efficient market structure.

These relationships develop in three time horizons: (i) the short term: it assumes that one of the production factors remains fixed; (ii) the near short term: it assumes that all production factors remain invariable; and (iii) the long term: all the production factors can be adjusted to maximize profit, that is, the firm can decide whether or not it wants to remain in its economic sector. Losses in the short term indicate that the firm can remain in the market trying to recover. However, in the long term, it should leave this market.

The long-run industry supply ($S(p)$) is the sum of the individual supplies of the n firms ($Si(p)$), as follows:

$$S(p) = \sum_{i=1}^{n} S_i(p) \tag{1.2.4}$$

Thus Eq. (1.2.4) is characterized by the exit of loss-making firms, the entry of firms expecting positive profits, market fluidity (as long as there are excess profits, the number of firms will increase), and the long-term stabilization of the break-even point. Additionally, there is only one price such that the quantity that firms wish to supply is the quantity demanded by consumers, i.e., there are no unsatisfied buyers or sellers. In the short-term equilibrium, the optimal price and quantity (p^*, Q^*) are found, while in the long term the number of optimal firms in the market (p^*, Q^*, n^*) is also considered.

Finally, in perfect competition, efficiency in the use of resources and the maximization of well-being are ensured.

1.2.3 Efficiency and Well-Being

The market economy, in free competition, is often considered by economists as the best way to organize economic activity, which implies it is the most effective method of allocating scarce resources for alternative purposes. The allocations in this case are efficient in the Pareto sense, which means it is not possible to improve the well-being of one individual without worsening that of another. In other words, this ideal equilibrium allows for the optimal allocation of resources, ensuring that each good is produced at the lowest possible cost and that the value assigned by consumers is equal to the marginal cost of production.

In a market economy, global economic activity stems from the decisions of many decentralized agents (companies, households, etc.) that interact on different markets. Economic agents pursue their interests, and the price of goods guides their production, sales, and purchase decisions. We attribute to this highly decentralized organization the decisions on resource allocation, the prosperity of Western economies, and the superiority of these economies over centralized socialist economies where the central planner decides on resource allocation (see the concept of the invisible hand of A. Smith and F. Hayek).

In this respect, production in equilibrium is efficient because all products are manufactured at a minimum cost, and the value that a buyer assigns to the consumption of a good is exactly equal to the marginal cost of producing of that good.

Welfare, on the other hand, is commonly associated with definitions of surplus, such as (i) ***consumer surplus***, the amount a consumer is willing to spend—if necessary—beyond the price to acquire a unit of output, i.e., the area below the demand curve and above the equilibrium price; (ii) ***producer surplus***, the amount of income the producer would give up without production being unprofitable, i.e., the area above the supply curve and below the equilibrium price.

On the other hand, government intervention, such as taxes, can generate welfare losses known as "deadweight losses." These represent the social cost of diverting resource allocation from competitive equilibrium. However, taxes can be justified if implemented efficiently to redistribute income or correct market failures. For example, suppose the government increases consumption taxes by T per unit sold, the government takes T, and the firm receives $p - T$. The tax creates a gap T between the value that the consumer of the last unit places on that unit and the cost that the

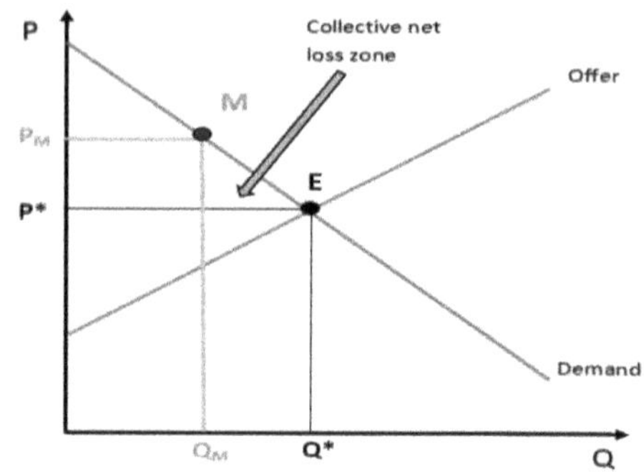

Fig. 1.2 Collective loss. Source: Author

supplier of that unit is willing to bear to produce it. The tax lowers the price that the firm receives; therefore, there is a reduction in supply, and at the same time, the price paid by the consumer increases. The tax is justified if it is used to redistribute income effectively. The tax incidence depends on the shapes of the supply and demand curves. The government can minimize the deadweight loss to society by taxing those products that are inelastic in supply or demand more heavily. If the supply curve is completely inelastic, the tax will not reduce output, so there will be no net loss. This effect can be seen in the following Fig. 1.2. In this context, although the theory of perfect competition offers an ideal framework for analyzing the market economy, reality shows that market power, externalities, and imperfections distort this equilibrium. These limitations underscore the importance of regulations and economic policies designed to bring markets closer to this ideal.

In contrast to theoretical models presented in this chapter, markets show different characteristics. For instance, markets are rarely perfectly competitive. Some firms have all the market power as buyers or sellers, which implies an innate ability to set prices. On the other hand, firms rarely offer the same goods; the differences may be linked to the characteristics of the goods or the location of the firms in the market. Firms do not enter markets freely, as there are natural or nonnatural barriers, and there are costs in entering and exiting the market. Furthermore, information can be incomplete and asymmetric; some economic agents are better informed than others. For these reasons, Industrial Organization is based not on perfect competition but on imperfect competition. The imperfect competition framework is suitable for studying oligopolistic competition (few firms in the market) or monopoly (only one supplier). These are situations faced by economic sectors, such as banking or telecommunications.

1.3 To Remember

1. Industrial Organization or Industrial Economics uses tools from microeconomics and perfects to analyze the market and the strategies of firms.
2. Schools of thought:
    a. The basic paradigm of the Harvard School is (Fig. 1.3):
    b. The Chicago school modifies the paradigm to **C**omportance, **P**erformance, **S**tructure.
    c. The new Industrial Economics considers the strategic behavior of the agents.
3. The interest of the perfect competition model is as follows:
    a. A reference for defining competition policy. The criteria used to assess competitiveness are the influence of companies on price, the significant number of companies, and market fluidity. In addition, in this model, profits tend to be zero.
    b. A reference for understanding firm strategies.

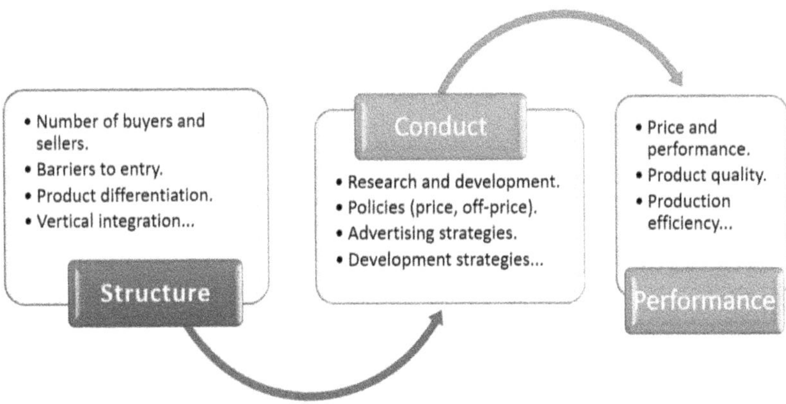

Fig. 1.3 S-C-P = basic paradigm in Industrial Economics. Source: Author

c. Allowing companies to understand the tools available to them to distance themselves from competition while retaining their customers. Companies then develop strategies to maintain competitive pressure, that is, to increase their market power and generate profits. Companies can do this through entry barriers, product homogeneity differentiation strategies, and information and transportation costs.

1.4 Suggested Questions

Choose the correct answer.

1. In a market economy, prices
   a. Are coordinated by the decisions of consumers and firms.
   b. Are different for consumers and firms.
   c. Are determined by firms.
   d. Are equal to costs.
2. Under perfect competition, which of the following conditions would result in the short-run marginal cost curve not correctly reflecting the supply behavior of a profit-maximizing firm?
   a. The firm is a price taker.
   b. Price exceeds the average total cost.
   c. The elasticity of demand facing the firm is 3.
   d. The elasticity of demand facing the firm is -3.
3. If price equals short-run average variable cost, the firm is at the point known as the:
   a. Revenue maximization point.
   b. Profit maximization.
   c. Closure.
   d. Profit minimization.
4. In a market economy, the price of a good:
   a. Is set by the government.
   b. Is set in the market.
   c. Is set by firms.
   d. Is set by consumers based on their demand.

5. The supply and demand curve:

   a. Is set by coordinated production and consumption decisions.
   b. Summarizes the optimal production and consumption decisions, respectively.
   c. Summarizes any production and consumption decisions, respectively.
   d. Indicates the scarcity of resources for production and consumption.

6. Demand curves shift because:

   a. Income changes.
   b. Prices of factors of production change.
   c. Technology changes.
   d. The number of producers changes.

7. A perfectly competitive industry will be in long-run equilibrium:

   a. When the number of firms is such that $P > MC = CP$.
   b. If there are no incentives for profit-maximizing firms to enter or exit the industry.
   c. When each firm operates at the maximum point on its long-run average cost curve.
   d. When there is no long-run equilibrium in a perfectly competitive industry

8. In a short-run competitive market, 60 firms operate, each with a cost function given by $CT = 12q + q^2$. The firm's supply curve is:

   a. $P = 10q$.
   b. $P = 30q$.
   c. $P = 6q$.
   d. $P = 60q$.

9. One night, Toribio decides to eat cannelloni (c) and a chocolate bar (b), according to the function $U(c, b) = 20\ ln(c) + 18\ ln(b)$. How many cannelloni and chocolate bars does he consume that night? (Cost is not a factor.) However, doctors have recently recommended that Toribio limit his consumption of cannelloni and chocolate to 5. How many cannelloni and chocolate bars will he consume under these new circumstances?

10. A perfectly competitive industry has many potential entrants. Each firm has the same cost structure so that the long-term average cost is minimized at a production level of 20 units ($q_i = 20$). The minimum average cost is 10 per unit. Total market demand is given by $Q = 1500 - 50P$. What is the long-run equilibrium price (P^*), total industry output (Q^*), and the number of firms?

PART I

Imperfect Structures

CHAPTER 2

Monopoly

In a monopoly, there is only a single seller, which benefits from price control. This implies that the monopolist acts as a price maker since it can determine the price of the good or service while adjusting its production level, unlike in perfectly competitive markets where companies are "price-takers." In principle, the reader will ask: *Why do they exist?* Among the reasons, we can list: (i) economies of scale, (ii) the behavior of companies, (iii) predatory behavior (***dumping***), (iv) control of a scarce resource or patent, and (v) the policy of public authorities.

(i) *Economies of scale:* We speak of economies of scale when the average total cost decreases as production increases. This phenomenon is typical of industries with high fixed costs and low variable costs, such as public transportation, telecommunications, or electricity generation. In this case, a company can produce relatively large quantities at a low average cost. In the case of economies of scale in certain industries, it leads to the disappearance of small companies, giving rise to a natural monopoly (a mechanism inherent to competition). For example, the cost of developing new software mainly depends on the initial design and development investment, whereas the cost of generating an extra copy is negligible. An additional example is the case of railway networks, where duplicating the infrastructure would be inefficient due to the high initial cost and limited physical space (Carlton and Perloff 2008). Another

C. Lanchimba, *Industrial Organization*,
https://doi.org/10.1007/978-3-032-10906-4_2

example is the automotive firm General Motors, which achieved first place in the category "Overall Workplace of Choice Result" at the 2023 Manufacturing Awards, demonstrating its ability to optimize resources by improving its productivity and increasing competitiveness by offering low prices, good quality, and service that meets customer expectations (General Motors 2023).

(ii) *The behavior of companies:* Different strategies for building barriers to entry can allow a company to create a monopoly. Similarly, controlling resources indispensable to manufacturing certain products can lead to a monopoly. For example, around 90% of Microsoft computers use the operating system produced by the same company. Instead of selling the Windows operating system and other packages it produces separately, Microsoft sells a comprehensive package that includes Windows and other software. Thus, the consumer has limited freedom when selecting software for its computer, as it comes with the Windows operating system. This situation illustrates not only the implementation of market control through vertical integration strategies but also how product bundling decisions can limit consumer choice and consolidate a firm's market position (Yvrande-Billon and Saussier 2004). A similar situation occurred in the mobile phone market in Mexico, where companies such as Telcel and Movistar compete strongly in their market. Their strategies to gain more market share include offers, promotions, alliances, advertising campaigns, and adopting new technologies new technologies to maintain a competitive advantage, which they present on their official websites and physical stores (Movistar 2024).

(iii) *Predatory behavior (dumping):* Consolidated large firms can afford to make temporary losses in a market by setting a price below (or equal to) its average total cost. Using this strategy, these firms drive its smaller or financially weaker competitors out of business. Once achieved, the firm can take advantage of its monopoly position to raise its prices and make more money than it previously lost. An example of this behavior is the strategy of large department stores when they set up where they are not as well-known as small local businesses. Another example is present in the digital platform services such as Amazon, which can take advantage of the low prices supported by other areas of their business to displace local competitors in specific markets. Once there is no competition, the firm can raise prices and recoup its losses, consolidating its market power. This practice has been widely documented and discussed in the economic literature (Baumol et al. 1982). Amazon provides another example as it entered the supermarket chain by acquiring Whole Foods Market, offering very low and attractive prices for its customers, which has caused its competitors such as Walmart and Kroger to lower their prices and invest in technology, which caused smaller chains such as Southeastern Grocers and Tops Friendly Markets to go bankrupt (Bloomberg 2018).

(iv) *Obtaining a patent:* A firm that develops a new product can obtain a patent to prevent its competitors from imitating it, which, in turn, would secure higher profits. For example, if a pharmaceutical company A is considering developing a new drug, this company A will produce it if it believes this project is profitable. However, drug development involves high financial risks and long research periods. Thus, the features of these markets underscore the importance of patents as incentives for innovation. For simplicity, let us imagine that people need 1000 units of this drug. For a price $p \leqslant 150$ per unit, consumers agree to buy 1000 units (i.e., the consumer is more satisfied when purchasing the product than when not purchasing it). Moreover, the costs of developing the drug are 90,000, and the other manufacturing costs are 10 per unit. If a firm develops the drug and produces 1,000 units, the production cost per unit produced equals $\frac{90{,}000+(10\times 1000)}{1000} = 100USD$. In this case, the project is profitable when the firm sells 10,000 units for between 100 and 150 USD. However, let's assume that imitating this drug and its manufacturing process is very easy (for simplicity, the cost of copying is zero). In this case, firm A knows that if it develops the drug, the following will happen: if it sells for $100 \leqslant p \leqslant 150$, another firm, say B, will copy drug A, produce it, and sell it at a lower price. Remember that firm A spent 90,000 on research. Therefore, the proposed development of the drug may not be profitable. Knowing this, firm A will refuse to develop the drug. Similarly, not all companies in the pharmaceutical sector with a similar reasoning will produce the drug either. As a result, the drug may not be created, and the

population may not benefit. Therefore, a patent law is justified.[1] This right protects companies that innovate. However, this exclusivity can also lead to the establishment of monopolistic prices, which poses a dilemma between encouraging innovation and ensuring accessibility to medicines (Schumpeter 1942). Similarly, not only do patents protect investments in innovation, but they also promote technology transfer through licensing agreements, contributing to economic and social development. An example is Apple, which that retains patents on key technologies for creating and designing its products. In this way, it protects its competitive advantage in the market and prevents its competition from using the same technology (Apple Inc 2024).

(v) *Government policy:* Some goods may be insufficiently produced, and their prices may be significantly high. Therefore, governments may therefore ensure the existence of a monopoly by allowing a single company to produce that good or service. That is the case of electricity in France and Ecuador. Such monopolies are called "state monopolies" and are usually subject to strict regulations to prevent price gouging and to ensure universal access to essential services. A government may also create a monopoly to protect a domestic producer from foreign competition by restrictions on trade, such as setting very high tariffs on imports. It may also regulate access to a profession, as in the case of notaries or pharmacies. In countries with complex legal systems, such as France, professional regulations ensure high standards of quality, but they also create barriers to entry that limit competition (Vickers and Yarrow 1988). For example, in Sweden, the sale of alcohol is regulated by allowing the purchase of alcoholic beverages only in government-controlled locations such as Systembolaget (Alex Smith 2021).

2.1 Producer of a Good with No Close Substitutes

The monopolist producer faces the challenge of maximizing its profits, considering that the price of its product depends on the quantity it decides

[1] Exclusive right to a product innovation, granting ownership for a period determined by the experts of the relevant authority.

to offer. In this context, the monopolist knows that by increasing the quantity produced, the supply will increase, leading to a decrease in the price. Thus, the market price is not a fixed parameter but depends on the interaction between supply and demand, which makes the monopolist a key agent capable of directly influencing the price of its product (Stiglitz 1987). The monopolist knows that his production affects the selling price; therefore, it must carefully choose the quantity Q that maximizes his profits. This decision is expressed as Eq. (2.1.1) through the following maximization problem:

$$max_Q \pi = R(Q) - C(Q), \tag{2.1.1}$$

where π is the producer's profit; R is the revenue from the sale of each unit produced, which is equal to the price $p(Q)$ times the quantity (Q); and C is the total cost of production of Q. To maximize the first-order condition is:

$$\frac{d\pi}{dQ} = MR - CM = 0 \Rightarrow MR = MC. \tag{2.1.2}$$

Therefore, we can conclude that, as in perfectly competitive markets, the monopolist's profits are maximized when marginal revenue (MR) equals marginal cost (MC). However, the key difference is that in a monopoly marginal revenue is always lower than the price of the good $(MR < P)$, which reflects the monopolist's market power to influence the price (Perloff, 2007). Graphically, the monopoly situation is represented as shown in Fig. 2.1.

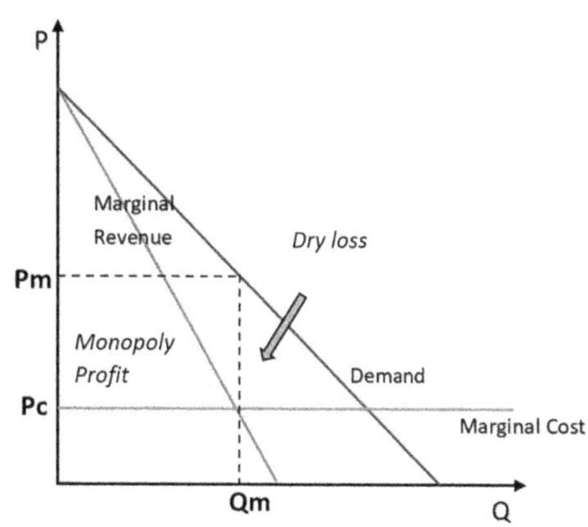

Fig. 2.1 Representation of Monopoly. Source: Author

If the monopolist does not lower its price to sell an additional unit, the increase in revenue associated with the sale would equal to the initial price. However, since the demand curve is downward sloping, the monopolist must lower the price to sell an additional unit, meaning that the selling price is greater than marginal revenue ($P > MR$). This phenomenon is key to understanding how monopolists determine prices compared to perfectly competitive markets. This relationship will be developed in more detail in Sect. 2.1.1.

Example 2.1 The inverse demand function of a monopoly is $p(q) = a - bq$ and its cost is $C(q) = cq^2 + A$. What are the monopolist's profits?

The profit function is given by $\pi(q) = (a - bq)q - cq^2 - A$. The monopolist chooses the quantity that maximizes its profits:

$$\frac{\delta\pi}{\delta q} = a - 2bq - 2cq \tag{2.1.3}$$

Solving for q from the (2.1.3) equation, we have: $q = \frac{a}{2(c+b)}$. Consequently, the monopoly price is: $p(q) = a - b(\frac{a}{2(c+b)}) = \frac{a(2c+b)}{2(c+b)}$. Replacing p and q in the profit function, we have: $\pi(q) = \frac{a^2}{4(c+b)} - A$. This example shows how the monopolist adjusts quantity and price according to its costs and the shape of the demand curve, allowing it to maximize its profits in a market without competition.

Example 2.2 Consider a monopolistic firm whose output level is $q \epsilon \mathbb{R}^+$. Suppose the inverse demand function is represented in Eq. (2.1.4):

$$p(q) = \begin{cases} \alpha - q & , if\ q \leq \alpha \\ 0 & , if\ q > \alpha \end{cases} \tag{2.1.4}$$

where p is the price. Both firms have a total cost of $C = \frac{3}{2}q$.

The firm maximizes its profits π (Eq. 2.1.5) are:

$$\pi_i(q) = \left(\alpha - q - \frac{3}{2}\right) q \tag{2.1.5}$$

$$\frac{\delta \pi_i(q)}{\delta q} = \alpha - 2q - \frac{3}{2}$$

The equilibrium quantity and price are represented in the Eq. (2.1.6). Suppose $\alpha > \frac{3}{2}$; otherwise, the profits are negative:

$$\left(q^* = \frac{2\alpha - 3}{4}, p^* = \frac{2\alpha + 3}{4}\right) \tag{2.1.6}$$

The profits of the monopolistic firm (Eq. 2.1.7) are:

$$\pi^* = \frac{(2\alpha - 3)^2}{16}. \tag{2.1.7}$$

This example illustrates how the costs and the shape of the demand curve affect a monopolist's output and pricing decisions, which in turn determines final profits.

2.1.1 *Pricing*

Marginal revenue is the profit from the sale of an additional unit, and it can be represented by the following equation:

$$MR = \frac{\Delta R}{\Delta Q} = \frac{\Delta PQ}{\Delta Q} \tag{2.1.8}$$

It is important to note that MR consists of two components: (i) the production and sale of an additional unit at price PPP, generating a marginal revenue of $MR = \frac{\Delta PQ}{\Delta Q} = \frac{P1}{1} = P$, and (ii) since the firm faces a downward-sloping demand curve, producing and selling this additional unit also lead to a price reduction, $\frac{\Delta P}{\Delta Q}$, which lowers the revenue from all previously sold units (change in revenue: $Q\frac{\Delta P}{\Delta Q}$). Consequently, marginal revenue is influenced not only by the sale of the additional unit but also by the price reduction affecting prior sales.

The total revenue Eq. (2.1.9) is expressed as:

$$R = PQ \Rightarrow \frac{\delta R}{\delta Q} = P + Q\left(\frac{\Delta P}{\Delta Q}\right) \tag{2.1.9}$$

$$MR = P + P\left(\frac{Q}{P}\right)\frac{\Delta P}{\Delta Q}. \tag{2.1.10}$$

As noted in Chap. 1, the elasticity of demand is defined in Eq. (2.1.11) as:

$$\epsilon_p = \left(\frac{\text{var } Q}{\text{var } P}\right)\left(\frac{P}{Q}\right). \tag{2.1.11}$$

Thus, $(\frac{Q}{P})(\frac{\Delta P}{\Delta Q})$ is the inverse of the elasticity of demand $\frac{1}{\epsilon_p}$, as measured by the revenue-maximizing quantity. Then MR in Eq. (2.1.12),

$$MR = P + P\left(\frac{1}{\epsilon_p}\right). \tag{2.1.12}$$

Due to the Eq. (2.1.2), we can write $P + P(\frac{1}{\epsilon_p}) = MC$, rearranged is:

$$\frac{P - MC}{P} = \left(\frac{1}{\epsilon_p}\right). \tag{2.1.13}$$

Equation (2.1.13) is the monopoly pricing principle, where the price is a function of marginal cost ($P = \frac{MC}{(1+\frac{1}{\epsilon_p})}$). For example, if the elasticity of demand is -4 and marginal cost is 9, then the monopoly price is 12 ($P = \frac{9}{1-\frac{1}{4}}$). On the other hand, Eq. (2.1.13) corresponds to the Lerner Index that we will see in Chap. 6. Consequently, the monopoly situation represents the maximum price that a firm can set.

As seen in monopoly, the price premium charged by the monopolist depends on the price elasticity of demand. Thus, the price premium charged by the monopolist is due to the elasticity of demand. Thus, if the elasticity is large, the price charged by the monopoly is close to the *MC*, and if the elasticity is low, the price charged by the monopoly is higher than the *MC*.

2.2 Discriminatory Monopoly

Price differences for the same good may arise due to heterogeneity in consumers' willingness to pay, leading firms to implement tariffs or price discrimination. This discrimination is based on selling the same product at different prices, adjusted to each consumer's willingness to pay. Consequently, the discriminating monopolist can segment the market according to consumer characteristics since it knows the demands of different groups. The necessary conditions for this discrimination are the following: (i) the firm must have significant market power; (ii) consumers must have different payment dispositions, and firms must be able to identify them directly or indirectly (e.g., through self-selection); and (iii) resale possibilities must be limited because either costs are high or resale restrictions exist like in the case of services.

In this context, suppose there are two types of demand: q_1 and q_2. The monopoly profits are

$$\pi(q_1, q_2) = p_1 q_1 + p_2 q_2 - C(q_1, q_2) \tag{2.2.1}$$

where p_i is the price of the good for demand $i : 1, 2$, $C(q_i) = cq_i$ is the firm's cost of production, and the inverse demand function is $p_i(q_i) = \alpha_i - q_i$. Suppose $\alpha_1 > \alpha_2$.

Replacing the values of cost and price in Eq. (2.2.1), we have that

$$\pi(q_1, q_2) = (\alpha_1 - q_1)q_1 + (\alpha_2 - q_2)q_2 - c(q_1 + q_2). \tag{2.2.2}$$

The monopoly needs to find the optimal quantity that maximizes its profits:

$$\frac{\delta\pi(q_1, q_2)}{\delta q_1} = \alpha_1 - 2q_1 - c$$

$$\frac{\delta\pi(q_1, q_2)}{\delta q_2} = \alpha_2 - 2q_2 - c$$

Consequently,

$$q_1 = \frac{\alpha_1 - c}{2}; \; p_1 = \frac{\alpha_1 + c}{2}$$

$$q_2 = \frac{\alpha_2 - c}{2}; \; p_2 = \frac{\alpha_2 + c}{2}.$$

Because $\alpha_1 > \alpha_2$, the quantity produced by the monopoly for demand 1 is greater than that for demand 2, and the reverse is true for prices.

Below are three types of discrimination that can be used. The difference between them is the degree of information required to discriminate consumers.

2.2.1 *First-Degree Discriminator*

First-degree discrimination, also known as perfect discrimination, involves extracting all consumer surplus. In other words, each consumer pays the maximum price they are willing to pay for the good, i.e., their reservation price. This type of discrimination requires the firm to have perfect information about each consumer's willingness to pay, which is extremely difficult to achieve in practice.

Figure 2.2 shows an example. Suppose that the only hotel in a city you have just arrived in has four rooms. The first person to take a room will pay the maximum price he is willing to pay, which is 50 USD, the second 40 USD, the third 30 USD, until the last person will pay 20 USD, which will correspond to marginal cost or the price of perfect competition. As a result, the hotel owner will have extracted all the surplus from the first three consumers.

This discrimination is practically impossible to carry out in real life because an individual's willingness to pay is private information that they

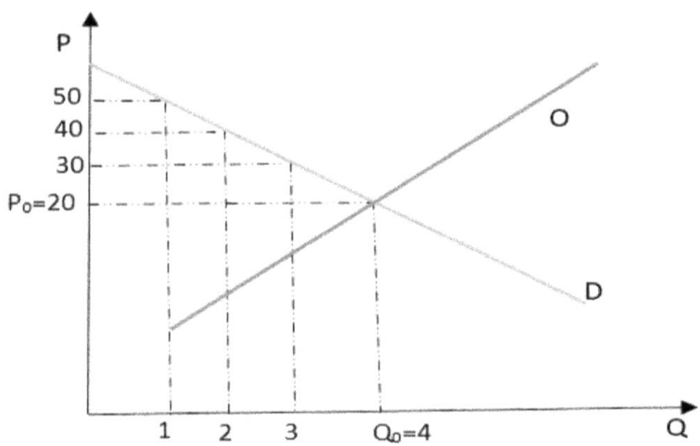

Fig. 2.2 Example of a first-degree price discriminator. Source: Author

are not willing to reveal. In the absence of perfect information, imperfect discrimination, such as second- or third-degree discrimination, can be used.

2.2.2 *Second-Degree Discriminator*

Second-degree discrimination, also known as list-price discrimination or volume-based pricing, relies on offering incentives for consumers to choose different price and quantity options. This type of discrimination does not require perfect information about each consumer. Instead, consumers self-select by choosing the options that best fit their willingness to pay.

The idea is that the firm offers a menu of price formulas associated with price and quantity. That is, the price tends to decrease with the amount consumed. Consumers choose from a menu the offer that best suits their consumption, causing consumers to reveal their willingness to pay. Consumers with the highest willingness to pay will choose the largest menu, while those with the least will choose the smallest. For example, the producer offers volume discounts, minimum purchases, fixed-amount payments, and tied selling.

A two-part linear tariff could consist of a fixed part a, to be paid by the producer regardless of the volume of purchases, and a part that would vary with the volume of purchase units q, which are offered at a price p. Consequently, this tariff $T(q)$ would be $T(q) = a + pq$. In this sense, the average price paid by the consumer would be $p = \frac{\frac{a}{q}}{p}$. This tariff is feasible when the average price is low. To set a, one should first look for a price that equals the marginal cost (perfect competition price) and look for an a that equals the consumer surplus.

2.2.3 *Third-Degree Discriminator*

Third-degree discrimination, also known as market separation discrimination, does not require knowledge of the demand curve for each consumer but instead focuses on segmenting consumers into homogeneous categories based on observable characteristics such as geographic region, season, or demographic traits. Common examples include price differentials between urban and rural markets or during different times of the year, such as holidays or the beginning of the school year. These segments typically have different price elasticities of demand.

For example, if the marginal cost is the same in both markets:

$$MC_i = MC_j$$

where MC is the marginal cost. We know that $MC = P(1 + \frac{1}{e})$, so

$$P_i\left(1 + \frac{1}{e_i}\right) = P_j\left(1 + \frac{1}{e_j}\right),$$

or in other words

$$\frac{P_i}{P_j} = \frac{1 + \frac{1}{e_j}}{1 + \frac{1}{e_i}} \tag{2.2.3}$$

where P is the price and e is the elasticity of demand. Equation (2.2.3) shows that, for the same good in two different markets, it is possible to set different prices for the same good in two different markets depending on the elasticity of each market.

Finally, these three forms of discrimination require a certain level of information on the preferences of the consumer; thus, first-degree discrimination requires more information than third-degree, and this needs more than the second-degree.

2.3 Monopoly and Welfare

Perfect competition is the market structure that is most beneficial to the consumer since they retain all their surplus at the time of purchase. In a perfectly competitive market, firms have no market power, and the price adjusts to marginal cost (MC), which maximizes social welfare. However, when we analyze the monopoly, we observe that the monopolist can set prices above marginal costs, which generates a net welfare loss for society. Among the arguments to defend the effectiveness of a monopoly, we can point out the following: (i) a natural monopoly can generate more affordable products than a competitive market and (ii) the Schumpeterian argument, which claims that large companies are more innovative than smaller ones. However, monopolies can lead to deadweight losses and rent-seeking behavior,[2] which causes inefficiency. Moreover, a monopoly's

[2] Rent-seeking occurs when a firm expends real resources to achieve a monopoly situation.

existence can have other economic and social implications, such as high prices and inefficiency associated with a lack of competition.

Although a monopoly may improve efficiency in certain areas, the inefficiency it creates, such as deadweight losses and rent-seeking behaviors, may surpass any gains in efficiency. The concept of deadweight loss refers to the loss of social welfare when the monopolist sets a price above marginal cost, which prevents some consumers who value the product above its cost of production from purchasing it. Furthermore, rent-seeking behavior, as Milgrom and Roberts (1992) point out, implies that firms expend resources on activities that do not contribute to the general welfare, such as investments to limit competition or influence government policies that favor their monopolistic position.

According to the theory of imperfect competition, any market structure that deviates from perfect competition results in inefficiency, as price moves away from marginal cost, resulting in a loss to society that cannot be recovered. In his analysis of deadweight loss, Posner (1975) argues that although estimates of the social cost of monopoly often underestimate the magnitude of inefficiency, regulatory policies must address this inefficiency to maximize collective welfare.

On the other hand, the Sherman Act (1890) states: "*Every person who shall attempt to monopolize, collude, or conspire with another person or persons, to monopolize any part of the trade or commerce…, shall be deemed guilty of a felony.*" (In other words, any person who monopolizes or attempts to monopolize, either individually or in conjunction with others, shall be deemed guilty of a felony.) This type of legislation reflects the government's concern about monopolistic practices and their impact on social welfare, which is often affected by the lack of competition in markets. To illustrate this, the following example is presented.

On the one hand, the consumer's utility is represented by: $U(q, p, m) = m - pq + u(q)$, where m represents the consumer's income. On the other hand, the firm's utility is given by $\pi(q) = pq - C(q)$.

Thus, collective welfare is given by:

$$W = U(q, p, m) + \pi(q) \tag{2.3.1}$$

$$W = m - pq + u(q) + pq - C(q)$$

$$W = m + u(q) - C(q).$$

Maximizing the expression (2.3.2), we have:

$$\frac{\delta W}{\delta q} = \frac{\delta u(q)}{\delta q} = MC. \tag{2.3.2}$$

Knowing that in consumer equilibrium $\frac{\delta u(q)}{\delta q} = p(q)$, we have $p(q) = MC$.

Consequently, for society to be in equilibrium, it is necessary that $p(q) = MC$, which is the condition of perfect competition. In a monopoly, this situation is not possible since, as has been mentioned throughout this chapter, $p(q) > MC$, the monopolist sets a price higher than marginal cost, which causes social welfare losses as production is lower than at a competitive price.

We will denote the market demand function by $D(p)$. We know that in equilibrium, marginal revenue equals marginal cost:

$$RM(q) = MC(q) \tag{2.3.3}$$

$$p(q) + p'(q)q = MC \tag{2.3.4}$$

Dividing the Eq. (2.3.3) by $p(q)$, we have

$$\frac{p(q) - MC(q)}{p(q)} = \frac{p'(q)q}{p(q)}. \tag{2.3.5}$$

Since the inverse demand function is the reciprocal of the demand function, we have $p'(q) = \frac{1}{q'(p)}$. Then,

$$\frac{p'(q)q}{p(q)} = \frac{1}{q'(p)} \frac{q}{p(q)} = \frac{1}{q'(p)\frac{p(q)}{q}} = \frac{1}{\varepsilon_p}. \tag{2.3.6}$$

Joining equations (2.3.6) and (2.3.5), we have that:

$$\frac{p(q) - MC(q)}{p(q)} = -\frac{1}{\varepsilon_p}. \tag{2.3.7}$$

In equilibrium, we find the Lerner index that measures market power, represented in Eq. (2.3.24), defined as the difference between price and marginal cost. This index is crucial to assess the monopolist's ability to set prices higher than those observed in a competitive market. Similarly, the producer's ability to deviate from marginal cost MC depends on the elasticity of demand; the lower it is, the higher the price charged by the monopolist. This concept is central to the theory of industrial organization, as it provides a quantitative measure of market power and its impact on social welfare (Tirole 1988).

Finally, monopoly has a positive impact on social welfare in certain contexts, since the monopolist can benefit from economies of scale (natural monopoly). In addition, it has incentives to innovate and invest in research and development. The fact that monopolistic firms can take advantage of economies of scale and the benefits of research and development is a frequent argument in defense of monopolies. However, these benefits must always be balanced against the social costs derived from the lack of competition (Schumpeter 1942).

On the other hand, a monopoly would negatively impact social welfare due to the following reasons: (i) low incentives to innovate; (ii) high costs incurred by the monopoly to establish or maintain its position (rent-seekers), including advertising expenditures to eliminate competitors' products, resources devoted to preventing the entry of new competitors, and efforts to influence regulatory authorities; and (iii) excessive resources devoted to competition in the context of patent competition. These costs represent a form of social inefficiency that may be even more harmful than the benefits derived from economies of scale and innovation.

2.4 Monopoly Regulation

The fundamental principle of monopoly regulation is to achieve allocative efficiency. This state of the economy is achieved when the willingness to pay for a unit of production is at least as high as its cost of production, i.e., its marginal cost equals its marginal benefit. In this sense, governments play a crucial role as regulators, intervening in the market to prevent abusive prices and promote a social balance that benefits general welfare. In the case of a monopoly, regulation is mainly oriented toward price control, seeking to reestablish imperfect competition as close as possible to the perfectly competitive market.

Suppose that $C(Q) = F + cQ$ is the cost of production, where (F) is the fixed cost, and c is the cost per unit multiplied by the quantity produced (Q). Furthermore, the effective price is $P = c$; this leads to a monopoly loss of $\Pi = -F$. So, we have a financial equilibrium problem, whose solution could be a subsidy to the firm.

The problem with subsidies is that the law often forbids them. Consequently, to obtain F, the regulator will impose a rate that will create a loss of efficiency as large as the one the law intended to eliminate. A transfer from the state budget to the regulated firms introduces the risk of "rent-seeking."

Consequently, social welfare is maximized under the restriction when the regulated firm reaches a financial equilibrium ($\Pi \geq 0$). In the case of a single-product producer, the solution is average cost pricing. Meanwhile, for a multiproduct monopoly, the solution is more complex since there are many combinations of prices (and quantities) such that the monopoly has zero profits.

One of the most advanced strategies for achieving efficiency in multiproduct monopolies is Ramsey-Boiteux pricing, which consists of maximizing social surplus under the constraint that the monopolistic firm must cover its fixed costs. This strategy seeks to establish tariffs that are not uniform but proportional to the inverse elasticity of demand for the products. More concretely, the applied tariffs should be higher for products with more inelastic demand and lower for products with more elastic demand (Boiteux 1956). This technique allows monopolies to recover fixed costs without overburdening the most price-sensitive consumers, balancing the firm's needs with social welfare. The Ramsey-Boiteux tariff design has the potential to balance the interests of consumers and monopolists, preventing the price from being so high that it causes a significant welfare loss for society.

This regulatory approach seeks to reduce market distortions and promote economic efficiency that not only considers the interests of the monopolist but also protects consumers and social welfare as a whole.

2.5 Dominant Firm with Competitive Edge

In this market structure, there is a dominant firm (leader), which is different from others because it sets the price when competing with other smaller companies called the fringe. In addition, it controls a significant market share.

The fringe comprises price-taking companies, where each one has a small market share, but they may collectively have control of a significant proportion of the market. This structure occurs in industries where one firm controls a large part of sales. Some examples cited in Carlton and Perloff (2008) are:

- Kodak—Photographic film market—65% market share.
- General Electric—Generator sales—61% market share.
- Hewlett-Packard—Printer market—59% market share.

Other examples are:

- Amazon—E-commerce—58.03%, United States (Statista 2024).
- Windows—Operating system market—72%, Global (Atanasof 2024).
- Bimbo—Packaged bread—99.3%, Mexico (Global de Marketing de Grupo Bimbo 2024)

In this context, the following aspects make a company a leader: (i) The costs of the leading company would be lower than those of the companies in the fringe. Leading companies are more efficient than the competition due to different factors, such as technological advantage. Moreover, the leading company may have more experience because it has been in the market for a long time. Therefore, it has had time to learn (acquire experience). In addition, it has the necessary size to benefit from economies of scale. (ii) The goods produced by the leading firm are superior to the competition in terms of differentiation, i.e., there is a reputation due to the intensity of advertising or the firm's time in the market. (iii) The leader may be a cartel, i.e., a group of companies that act collectively as a dominant firm to set prices or quantities in common.

2.5.1 *Price Setting by a Leading Firm*

Firms in the competitive fringe align themselves around the price set by the dominant firm. If all firms produce identical goods, the dominant firm sets a price that other firms accept as given. This market structure is similar to perfect competition because economic agents are price-takers.

However, the market power of the dominant firm may expire in the following situations: (i) the number of firms that can enter the industry increases competition; (ii) the difference in costs between the dominant firm and those in the band may decrease with the appearance of a firm with lower costs than those of the dominant one; thus, suppressing the power of the dominant firm, and (iii) a rapid incursion of new firms, which would increase competition.

2.5.1.1 *Barrier-to-Entry Model*

The barrier-to-entry model implies that, given the number of companies already in the market, no other firm could enter. These barriers, such as economies of scale, information costs, and exclusive property rights, are fundamental determinants that affect competition in the market (Tirole 1988). An example is the case of companies in the service sector that reach agreements to be profitable. For instance, in 2007, Apple agreed that it could only operate with the AT-T telephone network (Apple Inc 2007).

The working hypotheses for this model comprise five key aspects: (i) there is a firm whose size dominates all the others, thanks to its low production costs; (ii) all firms except the dominant firm are price takers and determine their output levels by equalizing marginal costs with the industry price (p), which implies that these firms operate in a perfectly competitive market in which they cannot influence prices; (iii) the number of firms (n) in the competitive segment is fixed; no additional entry can take place, due to the entry barriers mentioned above; (iv) the dominant firm knows the demand curve $D(p)$; furthermore, products are homogeneous, i.e., there is a single price, which ensures that competition in the market is based exclusively on price and not on differences in product quality; (v) the dominant firm knows the supply curve of the competitive segment $S(p)$, i.e. it can provide an output of the band for each price level.

In this case, the dominant firm determines the long-term residual demand curve on which the dominant firms compete. It also determines the procedure for maximizing the utility of the dominant firm.

Long-Term Residual Demand Curve

Figure 2.3a illustrates the behavior of a representative firm in the competitive band. In the supply curve of the representative firm in the segment (price-taker), $\bar{p}$ is the break-even point of each firm in the segment that has zero profits and is indifferent to produce. This point is the minimum equilibrium at which firms have no incentive to enter or exit the market in the long term. Below the long-term equilibrium band, firms in the segment cease their activity, and the dominant firm becomes a monopoly.

The supply curve of the competitive segment, $S(p)$, is the sum of the individual supply curves $S(p) = nq_f(p)$, where n is the number of firms in the segment and q_f is the production of a typical firm in the band. This representation reflects how competing firms offer a total quantity of goods at prices that allow them to cover their marginal costs.

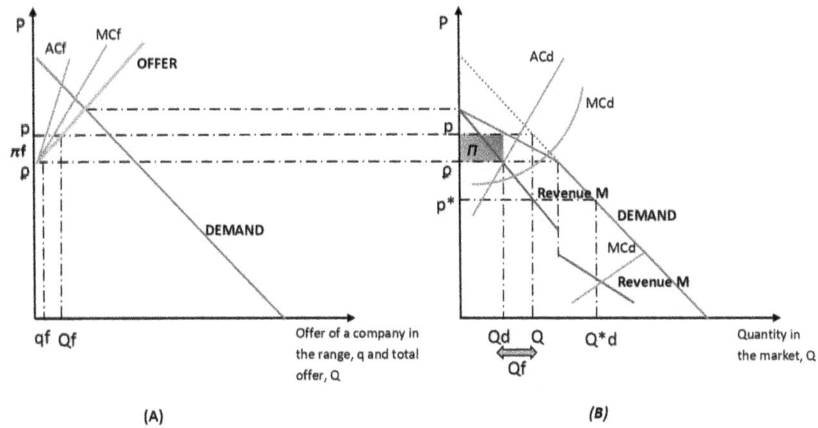

Fig. 2.3 Graphical representation of a model with barriers to entry. Source: Author

The dominant firm's long-run residual demand curve, $D_d(p)$, is the difference between the market demand curve and the band's supply curve; it is $D_d(p) = D(p) - S(p)$. This curve reflects that the dominant firm faces reduced demand as the band's competition adapts and behaves as a separate entity in the market.

On the other hand, in Fig. 2.3b, the market demand curve is the dotted line above the residual demand curve (solid line), suggesting that the price consumers are willing to pay exceeds the competing firms' cost of production. The two curves point out that the price is below the break-even point of the band's firms.

In this context, in Fig. 2.3, there could be two potential equilibria in Fig. 2.3a. The dominant firm chooses the price or output level that equals its marginal cost and marginal revenue. Its marginal revenue (MR) curve stems from the residual demand curve. The dominant firm asses the residual demand and behaves as a monopolist. This monopolistic behavior is consistent with the theory of profit maximization in pure monopolies (Carlton and Perloff 2008). The marginal revenue curve has two parts, i.e., two possible equilibria. Selecting one of the two equilibria depends on the cost curves of the dominant firm.

First Potential Equilibrium with Competitive Fringe In this case, the costs of the dominant firms are close to those of the fringe firms. The dominant firm sets a high price, derived from profits, that equals those of the fringe firm. However, unlike the fringe firms, the dominant firm has a greater capacity to influence the price due to its size and efficiency, which allows it to maximize its profits

Figure 2.3b shows the marginal cost (MC). The dominant firm chooses the production level Q_d and the price p. The difference between the market demand Q and the production of the dominant firm Q_d is equal to the competitive fringe supply Q_f. In addition, the utility of the dominant firm is π. In this case, the profit of a typical fringe firm is π_f (A). Hence, $\pi > \pi_f$ because the dominant firm's average cost is higher than the fringe's.

In this version of the model, when the dominant firm lowers its price, the fringe does the same. For example, in the market for PC processors, the competition consists of a fringe of three firms where Intel has a market share that makes it dominant. If one of the fringe firms (Intel) suddenly lowers its price by 70%, its competitors followed suit in their strategy of lowering prices within 2 days. On the other hand, the dominant firm has a monopoly profit because it has lower costs than the fringe. However, the price is slightly lower due to the presence of the fringe; this translates into a benefit to consumers.

Second Potential Equilibrium Dominant Firm Becomes Monopoly If the costs of the dominant firm are lower than those of the firms in the strip, the dominant firm sets a price below the long-run profitability threshold of the firms in this segment and eliminates all competition. Figure 2.3b shows the marginal cost curve $= MC_d^*$. The dominant firm chooses the production level Q_d^* and the price p^*. Consequently, it becomes a monopoly.

2.5.1.2 Model with Market Fluidity

A more realistic alternative to the model without fluidity is when firms can enter and leave the market freely. In this case, the firms in the strip cannot generate profits in the long run either because they operate at the profitability threshold or close(contestability). In this case, the dominant firm cannot set a price higher than the previous model. Their costs are lower than those of the companies in the strip; therefore, their utility is positive but lower than in the case of barriers to entry.

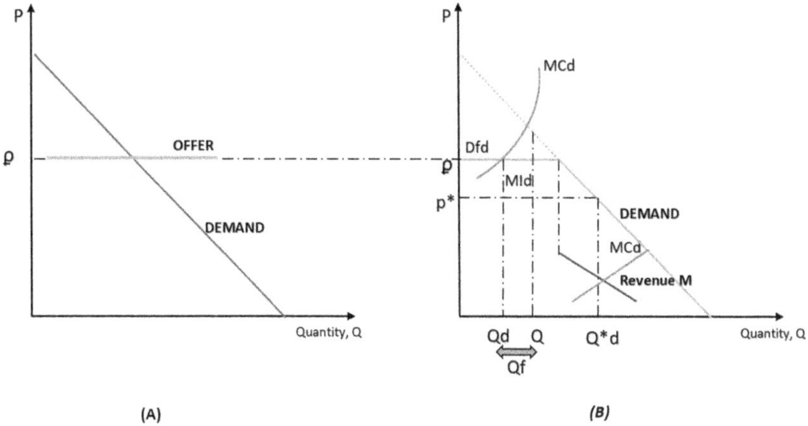

Fig. 2.4 Graphical representation of a model without barriers to entry. Source: Author

In Fig. 2.4a, the supply of the strip is a horizontal line at the profitability threshold (minimum of average cost), while in Fig. 2.4b there is a choice of the dominant firm and market equilibrium.

The residual demand curve is horizontal at the profitability threshold of the firms in competitive segment. Thus, its marginal revenue curve is horizontal (horizontal demand curve) as in perfect competition. This relationship implies that price equals marginal revenue ($p = MR$). Therefore, there would be two possible equilibria: (i) if the marginal cost of the dominant firm (MC_d) is high and cuts the marginal revenue curve in its horizontal part. In addition, the price is equal to the closing threshold of the firms in the strip. Then, the quantity produced by the strip depends on the cost of the structure of the dominant firm, the production level Q_d, and the price p; (ii) the mere threat of entry keeps the price at the break-even point of the firms in the band. As a result, the dominant firm becomes a monopoly because its production costs are much lower than those of the band. In this case, the threat of entry is not credible and sets a price below the break-even point of the firms in the band, and the dominant firm eliminates all competition and becomes a monopoly.

2.6 To Remember

1. The most profitable level of production for the monopolist is the one where marginal revenue equals marginal cost.
2. The profitability of the monopolist depends on the relationship between price and average cost.
3. Monopolistic producers can choose different quality levels.
4. A monopolist who discriminates by price could obtain, in the case of the first-degree discriminator, all the consumer surplus.
5. Monopolies are not necessarily bad, since in some cases they are more efficient than several firms producing.
6. The dominant firm in a competitive market is not a monopoly. However, it behaves as if it were one in terms of its share of demand.

2.7 Suggested Questions

Answer the following questions:

1. Suppose that Mr. Camilo Lopez is the only producer of televisions: Is he guaranteed to always make a profit?
    a. Monopolies do not always make a profit.
    b. Monopolies always make a profit.
    c. If demand is close to zero.
    d. If their marginal costs are extremely high and demand is low.
2. Which of the following is a characteristic of a monopoly?
    a. Few firms in the market.
    b. Easy entry and exit.
    c. No barriers to entry.
    d. Only one firm in the market.
3. Which of the following can create a monopoly?
    I. High prices.
    II. Patent.
    III. Government license.
    IV. Exclusive distribution of a good.

    a. I and II.
    b. I and III.

c. I, II, and III.
d. II, III, and IV.

4. Compared to a competitive market, a monopoly:

   a. Offers a larger quantity
   b. Generates greater consumer surplus
   c. Reduces the quantity supplied and raises prices
   d. Improves Pareto efficiency

5. Select the type of market in which all firms sell identical products; neither buyers nor sellers can influence the price.

   a. Perfect competition.
   b. Oligopoly.
   c. Monopolistic competition.
   d. Monopoly.

6. Which of the following statements is true at the optimal output level of a monopoly?

   a. Price equals marginal revenue.
   b. Price is greater than marginal cost.
   c. Average cost is less than marginal cost.
   d. Marginal cost is zero.

7. A firm's marginal cost is defined as:

   a. The ratio of total cost to total output.
   b. The ratio of total output to total cost.
   c. The additional cost of producing one more unit of output.
   d. Wage cost.

8. Price discrimination refers to the ability to

   a. Sell identical products at different prices.
   b. Sell a homogeneous good everywhere at the same price.
   c. Sell different types of goods at different prices.
   d. Sell different types of goods at the same price.

9. Suppose a perfectly competitive industry produces candles at a constant marginal cost of \$10 per unit. Marginal costs when monopoly is established increase to \$12 per unit because \$2 must be paid to other groups

to maintain the monopoly position. Suppose the market demand for these candles is determined by $QD = 1000 - 50P$.

a. Calculate the level of output and prices under perfect competition.
b. Calculate the level of output and prices under monopolization.
c. Calculate the total loss in consumer surplus under monopolization of appliance production.
d. Calculate the deadweight loss (use a graph).

10. Solve: A monopolist has to decide how to allocate its output between two geographically separated markets. The demand and marginal revenue for the two markets are $P_1 = 15 - Q_1$; $MR_1 = 15 - 2Q_1$ and $P_2 = 25 - 2Q_2$; $MR_2 = 25 - 4Q_2$. The monopolist's total cost is $C = 5 + 3(Q_1 + Q_2)$. Determine the market price, the level of production, and the profits if

    a. It is a pure monopolist.
    b. The monopolist can practice price discrimination by splitting markets.

CHAPTER 3

The Differentiation

One way to reduce competition between firms is to reduce substitutability, which is achieved when products are different. As a result of this strategy, consumers no longer consider price as the sole criterion for choice, as they value product characteristics and consumer preferences, which change the intensity of competition. This type of product differentiation is often associated with monopolistic competition, so we will begin by describing this market structure. Subsequently, we will discuss vertical and horizontal product differentiation to complete advertising as a differentiation tool.

3.1 Monopolistic Competition

Monopolistic competition is a hybrid competition regime between monopoly and perfect competition. This type of market has three distinctive features: the existence of many firms, free entry (competition), and monopolistic production of a product variation by each firm. In other words, each firm has its customers, that is, it has a share of the demand (residual demand). The importance of the customer depends on the number of competitors in the market and the degree of differentiation of their products.

In this type of market, each firm considers the prices of its competitors as given. Therefore, it ignores the impact of its price on the other companies,

C. Lanchimba, *Industrial Organization*,
https://doi.org/10.1007/978-3-032-10906-4_3

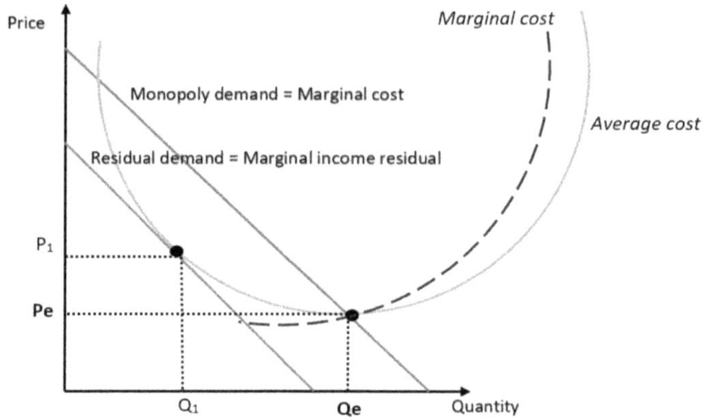

Fig. 3.1 Monopolistic competition equilibrium. Source: Author

that is, it does not have strategic behavior due to the large number of competitors in the market.

As in perfect competition, the economic profits for producers are zero under monopolistic competition. In contrast, the slope of the demand in monopolistic competition is horizontal; thus, it differs from the downward-sloping demand curve in perfect competition. Furthermore, perfect competition is different from monopolistic competition since demand has a downward slope, unlike perfect competition, where it is horizontal. Furthermore, monopolistic competition is different from oligopoly with price competition, since a change in the price of a single company has a negligible effect on the demand of any other. Finally, companies in monopolistic competition have market power, which implies the possibility of selling at a price above marginal cost. This situation occurs because there is a residual demand with consumers willing to pay more. As a result, market niches appear, but the long-term benefits are zero due to product market fluidity.

Figure 3.1 shows the perfect competition equilibrium (P_e, Q_e). Monopoly demand decreases because it has a downward slope, which expresses market power. Residual demand shows the agents who could pay a little more for a product. However, market fluidity generates zero profits in the long run. Thus, the equilibrium of monopolistic competition is the point of tangency between residual demand and the average cost curve (P_1, Q_1). As a result, the price is higher in monopolistic competition compared to perfect competition because there are fewer firms. Consequently, market power in this market structure does not necessarily translate into extra profit for the producer.

3.2 Product Differentiation

A question that may arise when observing the market is as follows: *Why are consumers willing to pay more for certain products?* In fact, the answer is quite simple. Consumers would be willing to pay more for some products due to their differentiation, which is often associated with monopolistic competition. The first works that study the impact of differentiation on the behavior of sellers and buyers are Chamberlin (1933), Robinson (1934), and Hotelling (1929).

In this sense, Chamberlin (1933) points out that "a general category of product is differentiated if there is a *sufficient basis* to *distinguish* the products of one seller from those of another. It does not matter whether this basis is *real* or *illusory*, as long as it has some *importance* to buyers and leads to the preference for a variety of products."

Therefore, the market study of differentiated products is based on two key concepts. First, products are differentiated only to the extent that consumers think they are different, i.e., "the consumer is always right." For example, two chemically identical brands of aspirin brands are differentiated products if consumers consider them as such. Likewise, between Coca-Cola and Pepsi-Cola, only 37% of loyal consumers can recognize the brand they intend to prefer (Carlton and Perloff 2008). Second, if the price of one brand has a strong effect on another brand's price, the companies are *direct competitors*, which implies both brands are closely substitutable. For example, wheat is a homogeneous product. Consumers are indifferent to the farm from which a particular sack of wheat comes. Plumbers in a small town are another example where consumers are indifferent.

Therefore, a firm's products are homogeneous when consumers do not attach importance to the brand they buy. Economists distinguish two main forms of differentiation: horizontal and vertical.

3.2.1 Horizontal Differentiation

This type of differentiation refers to subjective taste characteristics among consumers, where preferences are in the same category as the product's characteristics.

In the consumer theory developed by Lancaster (1966, 1971, 1979), consumer preferences depend on the characteristics of goods. Moreover, each good can be represented by a set of features. For example, we can define a set of characteristics, such as softness, temperature, etc., to analyze ice cream and candy as two different sets. To illustrate how products can be compared by examining their characteristics, suppose that the only important characteristic of a soft drink is its sweetness. In this case, different soft drinks can be classified on a scale of "sweetness," which goes from "not sweet at all" to "very sweet." On this scale, for example, Sprite would be classified to the left of regular Coca-Cola, which would be to the left of Pepsi. Moreover, we can classify products in feature space with several dimensions, each dimension (axis) representing an attribute. Another example is the Fiat Punto and the Ford Fiesta, which belong to the same segment of compact cars but are differentiated by the brand that manufactures them (Ultimate Specs 2002).

Two competing products in the same market are differentiated horizontally when, at identical prices, consumers have different preferences for them. Therefore, there is no *unanimous ranking*. Horizontal differentiation also refers, for example, to a spatial differentiation of companies as proposed in the Hotelling's model (1929).

Another point is that companies often combine different product characteristics (design, shape, colors, etc.). This constitutes another form of horizontal differentiation, which depends on the heterogeneity of consumer preferences or tastes. For their part, consumers tend to disagree on the features of the "ideal" product since some prefer a modern design, while others prefer a more traditional one. In this context, consumers buy what most closely resembles what they understand as ideal. On the other hand, location models, where location can be part of the product characteristics, are a mechanism that can help us better understand horizontal differentiation.

3.2.1.1 Location Models

Spatial competition, where customer behaviors are influenced by transportation costs and the relative locations of buyers and suppliers, can give rise to multiple retail location patterns. Outlet agglomeration is one of the most relevant. Contrary to spatial competition in standard microeconomic models, spatial competition has monopolistic features that lead to agglomeration. Space introduces monopolistic elements, and as in spatial markets, all firms enjoy some degree of monopoly power over their immediate market area. In this analytical context, the pioneering contribution of Hotelling (1929) formally demonstrates the benefits of clustering.

Hotelling's Model Hotelling (1929) developed a model that explains companies' location, behavior, and pricing in a geographic area, in which location is a distinctive characteristic of consumers and companies.

The Hotelling's model or "linear city model" shows that in a maximizing duopoly, firms secure their market share when they sell identical products from fixed locations in a bounded linear market, especially when they cluster in the center of the market area. Thus, the modeled non-collusive duopolistic competition leads to price stability and is characterized by the principle of minimum differentiation. This demonstration can be extended to various types of locations other than spatial, such as location in terms of product differences. However, Hotelling's analysis stands out as the main normative theory of retail location and the principle of minimum differentiation as the most relevant explanation of the agglomeration of similar retail firms.

In Hotelling's location model, the consumer must consider factors other than the price, such as the opportunity cost of going to a specific seller (or the delivery cost of the good). The cost increases with the distance between the buyer and the seller (transportation costs). In other words, the product difference only depends on the store location. The consumer will choose the nearest seller for the same good, so location leads to differences in consumer preferences. On the other hand, each seller has a certain market power over consumers who are close to it.

Lancaster (1966) and other economists have shown that this model could also be applied to the study of products that differ in several dimensions. Therefore, this model would also serve to study monopolistic competition if we consider that products are identified by their *position* in a *feature space*.

Let us assume Hotelling's model for a linear city built around a single main street, very long but of fixed size, where consumers are distributed uniformly along the main street. Apart from their location, consumers

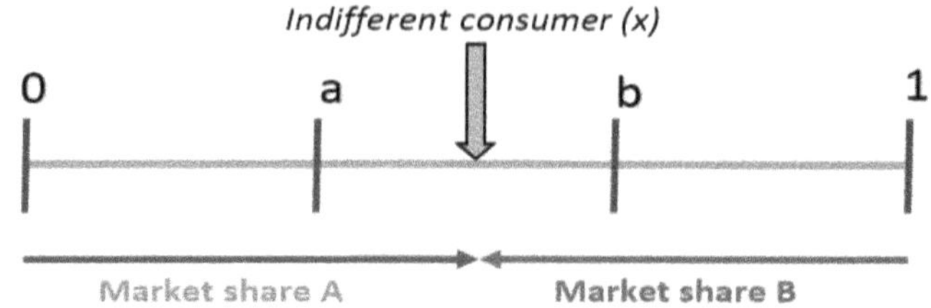

Fig. 3.2 Illustration of the linear city. Source: Author

are identical. In this city, there are two competing firms, A and B. This competition depends on quantity (no price competition due to the market maturity). On the other hand, to acquire the good, consumers must pay the price of the good and a transportation cost proportional to the distance: $T = t.l$. Thus, the location strategy determines the market share. In addition, each firm knows the set of possible locations but does not observe the location of its competitor. Therefore, it is a noncooperative location game (where firms simultaneously choose their location).

Thus, the model seeks the location equilibrium, that is, (i) *Where will firms choose to set up*? or (ii) *What product will they select to sell to have maximum demand*?. Moreover, we assume that firms A and B choose locations a and b, respectively. Therefore, to find the equilibrium, we need to find the demand for A and B when the prices are fixed and transportation costs are linear: $T(l) = t.l$.

In Fig. 3.2, it is shown that the consumer is indifferent to the point at which he is located; thus, he remains in x. The attraction zone of A is demand $D_a = x$, while the attraction zone of B is demand $D_b = (1 - x)$. The demand, according to the location, would be divided into $D_a = \frac{a+b}{2}$ and $D_b = 1 - \frac{a+b}{2}$. Then, the profit functions can be expressed as the following:

$$\pi_A = p.\left[\frac{a+b}{2}\right] \; y \; \pi_B = p.\left[1 - \frac{a+b}{2}\right]$$

The closer the space occupied by a is to the center, the larger the profit of the firm A. Therefore, A has an interest in getting closer to B. However, A wants to keep its market share on the left and invade the territory of B. Similarly, the more b decreases its proximity to the center, the more substantial the profit of the firm B is. Consequently, B has an incentive to get closer to "A," keeping its market share on the right and invading the territory of *A*.

In equilibrium, the two firms will have the same proportion of the market, $a = b = 1/2$, that is, there is a "minimum differentiation strategy." For fixed prices and linear transport costs, the two firms are in the average equilibrium (minimum differentiation). Each firm tries to locate in this place because, without price competition, the aim is to have a maximum market share. This situation would explain the fact that companies frequently choose nearby locations.

An example of a minimum differentiation strategy is McDonald's competition around the world without doing any market research. A fast-food chain's choice of location is necessarily close to an existing establishment. This is a leader-follower strategy, that is, a Stackelberg oligopoly and a minimum differentiation strategy.

Some variants of this model are the following:

- Companies that select both location and price. Companies choose between two alternatives: (i) they choose a strong differentiation and a low impact on the sales price competition, so they gain on price but lose market share, and (ii) they choose a low differentiation to increase their market share, but the impact on competition is significant. Consequently, they gain in sales volume but lose on price.
- If firms are located in the same location, $a = b$, then the difference in equilibrium prices is zero.
- If firms are maximally differentiating, firms expand to form local monopolies that mitigate the price competition they have. An example of this market structure is car manufacturers like Ferrari and Clio.
- If firms are at either end of the segment $a = 0$ and $b = 1$, then prices are high. In this case, firms are maximally differentiating, and the effect of competition is minimal, but there is a decrease in market share due to high prices.

A business example based on Hotelling's model is the strategy of physical stores such as 7-Eleven, which introduces premium products under its own brand and allows it to capture more customer niches. Furthermore, it minimizes the distance costs perceived by customers to purchase exclusive products (Chai et al. 2020).

Circle Model Unlike the Hotelling's model, this model assumes that the city is not linear. The idea is that the center is not accessible. An example

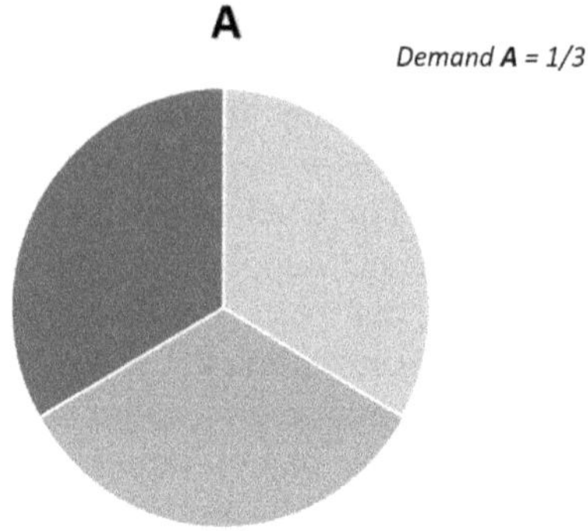

Fig. 3.3 Illustration of the city in a circle. Source: Author

of this market structure is a regulation prohibiting certain economic activities in the city center (liquor factories, weapons factories, etc.). The model is based on the following working hypotheses: (i) consumers are located uniformly on a circle with a diameter equal to one; (ii) there are transportation costs; (iii) in this case, the space produced is completely uniform, which implies that for any firm, no location is a priori better than another; and (iv) all travel is done along the circle since passing through the city center is expensive or prohibited. This is illustrated in Fig. 3.3.

In this model, equilibrium occurs when the firms' market participation strategy is to position themselves equidistantly in the circle ($n > 2$). Therefore, the principle of maximum differentiation applies.

When n firms are equidistant, the equilibrium price will increase with the cost of transportation (t). Likewise, when the cost of transportation is high, the principle of local monopoly is applicable. On the other hand, competition from other firms decreases when each firm sells its product at a price above marginal cost. Conversely, when the value of t is low, the equilibrium price is close to the competitive price. Therefore, the more firms enter the market, the more prices decrease.

Thus, the choice of firms in terms of spatial location or positioning of their supply would be motivated by the generation of large profits and by obtaining a large market share. However, these two objectives may be conflicting, since a high generation of profits may lead to trying to retain a type of client (differentiation), thus moving away from competitors; the other involves getting closer to competitors to gain a larger market share. In this sense, if all companies were to adopt this behavior, companies would find themselves with identical positioning and intense competition.

Finally, it is important to highlight that this type of analysis has limitations when it comes to a chain that wants to choose locations for its retailers since there is a risk of cannibalization (Pancras et al. 2012). The cannibalization risk of the location is related to spatial competition between geographically close retail outlets when the presence of a new unit captures the sales of other outlets. Consequently, the cannibalization effect impacts the spatial business choice of the chains. This intra-chain competition effect can influence spatial choices between dispersion.

An example that fits the circle model is the business model of Coca-Cola and Pepsi, where both occupy the same market space but strive to attract different consumers using marketing strategies. Coca-Cola focuses on family, happiness, and tradition, while Pepsi seeks to connect with young people, associating itself with music and sports (Brito-Rhor and Borja 2015).

3.2.2 *Vertical Differentiation*

Two goods competing in the same market are vertically differentiated when, at the same price, all consumers prefer one of them. Differentiation through quality illustrates this strategy, i.e., at an identical price, consumers prefer one good of superior quality to another, which implies all consumers agree on the ranking of the products.

Therefore, we assume that vertically differentiated products coexist in the market, and lower quality products are sold cheaper than better quality products.

Firms choose their vertical positioning by considering consumers' willingness to pay for quality and the cost of producing it. In a monopoly, for example, the firm will choose an optimal quality level to maximize its profits. If consumers are high-income, the firm will choose to make quality goods, which can be very high if the additional cost of higher quality is more than offset by the additional benefits. If consumers are heterogeneous in their preferences, the firm may decide to offer variants or versions of different quality, with a low price for the basic version and a higher price for the high-end one.

Thus, the quality of products determines vertical differentiation. Moreover, price differences justify the simultaneous existence of good and poor-quality products. Vertical differentiation models show that firms also prefer differentiation to reduce price competition. Vertical differentiation is considered maximum differentiation. However, each firm prefers to produce the highest quality.

Finally, when a firm's product is differentiated, its demand curve slopes downward, unlike that of a perfectly competitive price-taking firm, where demand is horizontal. Furthermore, the greater the product differentiation, the steeper the demand curve becomes due to a larger residual demand, ultimately giving the firm monopoly power. A monopoly is comparable to a firm whose product has no close substitutes.

3.2.3 *Advertising as a Tool of Differentiation*

Advertising is a differentiation tool because it distances the firm from the competition. Moving away from price competition creates market niches and exploits a monopoly power in these. The problem sometimes arises due to the nature of the product since sometimes differentiation is not possible. In this case, companies usually make tied sales,[1] in addition to other tools that will be described in this section. In this context, advertising as a differentiation tool has two opposing views that coexist in economic analysis.

The favorable view holds that advertising is a piece of information that facilitates rational choice for consumers by reducing search costs. This dynamic occurs because advertising announces the existence of a product, given its price, and describes its quality. Thus, advertising improves competition, guaranteeing market transparency. The unfavorable view, on the other hand, emphasizes that advertising is seen as a way of deceiving the consumer since it is a source of fictitious differentiation. In this sense, it would create barriers to entry.

Researchers in the area maintain that these two views are true to some extent. Similarly, two types of advertising are distinguished: informative and persuasive. Before addressing these concepts, it is first necessary to distinguish two types of goods (Nelson 1970 and Nelson 1974):

Search goods: For these types of goods, consumers must search for information about sellers and prices since they can observe the quality of these goods before buying them. If consumers have different search

[1] Tied sales occur when a firm conditions the sale or contracting of a product by the purchase or contracting of another product or service, such as a mortgage loan, for which life or unemployment insurance is sold.

costs, different prices may coexist in a market. For example, certain companies may choose high prices to make large profits, even though this will only attract consumers with high search costs, who will only visit a few companies.

Experience goods: Goods whose quality characteristics cannot be observed before purchase. Therefore, the quality of the good is known to the consumer only when the product has been tested, such as books, certain food products, or cosmetics.

According to Nelson, the nature of an "experience good" depends on the cost consumers incur when searching for information about its quality. In this context, a distinction is made between hard information (*hard*), which provides direct details about a product's existence, price, distribution, and characteristics (direct information) and soft information (*soft*), which conveys indirect information.

The distinction between search goods and experience goods leads to distinguishing two forms of advertising: *informative advertising*, which provides information about the characteristics of the product to reveal an objective differentiation, and *persuasive advertising*, which tries to change consumer preferences to create a subjective differentiation.

According to Nelson (1978), the informative form of advertising is the most common. This strategy is used for experience goods since the proportion of sales advertising is three times greater than for search goods. On the other hand, there are differences between informative advertising and persuasive advertising in terms of social welfare. Informative advertising has a priori value, while persuasive advertising has a less clear value.

In this context, the US Congress launched an accelerated approval process for generic drugs in 1984. Between 1984 and 1998, their market share increased from 18 to 42%. However, the price of branded drugs has not decreased but increased. This dynamic is mainly explained by the intensive advertising campaigns of the laboratories that distribute branded drugs, which would be in line with the idea of persuasive advertising.

On the other hand, for experience goods, it can be difficult to make informative advertising. However, advertising can be used to send a signal to consumers that the quality of a product is high. Let us suppose that there are low- and high-quality (experience) goods and that purchases are repetitive. Producers of high-quality goods may have strong incentives to spend large sums of money on advertising to signal themselves as a high-quality producer.[2] The underlying idea is that spending a lot is only rational if the firm offers a high-quality product.

The condition for this strategy to be credible is that a high-quality firm must be more interested in getting its product tried than a low-quality firm. This strategy is profitable because the equilibrium with advertising can be more effective than without it. However, the intensity of advertising expenditures (ratio of advertising to sales) varies across industries. For example, the ratio in the salt industry is 0–0.5%, while that for breakfast cereals ranges from 8 to 13%.

The Dorfman-Steiner formula (Dorfman and Steiner 1954) provides an explanation,

$$\frac{A}{R} = \frac{p - MC}{p}\eta = \frac{\eta}{\varepsilon}$$

where p is the price of the good, MC is the marginal cost. η represents the elasticity of demand for advertising expenditures, ε represents the price elasticity of demand, A is the amount of investment in advertising, and R is the income. An example is the following:

- Instant coffee: $(\varsigma/e) = 0.019$ and $(a/R) = 0.020$
- Beer bottle: $(\varsigma/e) = 0.008$ and $(a/R) = 0.011$
- Cigarettes: $(\varsigma/e) = 0.019$ and $(a/R) = 0.046$
- Soap: $(\varsigma/e) = 0.013$ and $(a/R) = 0.012$

We can apply the Dorfman-Steiner formula to get an intuition of the effect of market structure on the intensity of advertising investment. However, the price elasticity of firm demand varies depending on the number of competing firms, that is, it tends to increase with the number of firms present in the market. Therefore, the intensity of advertising tends to decrease.

On the other hand, the effect of an increase in the number of firms on η of a public good can lead to greater advertising, which, in turn, increases the demand for each firm. In this sense, the elasticity of advertising (and therefore the intensity of advertising) decreases with the number of firms.

An example of this was Nike's "Just Do It" campaign, launched in 1998, which used three words to connect with consumers by focusing

[2] Sending signals to consumers is known as signaling theory, which will be discussed in Chap. 5.

on motivation and self-improvement. Instead of highlighting product features, Nike differentiated itself by appealing to its customers' values, positioning it as a leader in the sports industry (Estudio 2024).

The Intensity of Advertising Expenditures on Public Goods Non-rivalry implies that the consumption of a good by one agent does not prevent its consumption by another (agents are not rivals for the consumption of the good). For example, the fact that an economic agent breathes does not deprive another agent of doing so. Nonexclusivity assumes that all agents have free access to a good, such as a water well. Therefore, advertising on this type of goods is informative.

If, on the contrary, the only effect of advertising is to switch consumers from one firm to another, then the only impact of advertising is to change consumers from one firm to another. A priori, the elasticity of advertising, and therefore the intensity of advertising, may increase with the number of firms, i.e., the incentives to capture the market from rival firms increase with the number of competing firms. This analysis suggests an ambiguous relationship between the intensity of advertising investment and the number of firms.

Empirical studies suggest that starting with a small number of firms, an increase in the number of firms will increase the intensity of the advertising intensity. Likewise, starting with a large number of firms, the number of firms will decrease with the intensity of advertising.

In general, advertising is an instrument of competition, like price. For example, if the only purpose of advertising is to move market share, it would be a "Bertrand" mechanism, where increasing advertising expenditures would rise until profits are zero.

However, advertising is distinguished from price because interactions between firms are less frequent. In addition, advertising is an investment that can have long-term effects.

3.2.3.1 Price and Advertising in Competition

Suppose Hotelling competition, i.e., linear differentiation, where the two firms are at the two extremes of the range of varieties. Consumers are uniformly distributed over the interval. However, they are assumed to be unaware of the differences between the two firms' goods. In this sense, there would be "Bertrand' competition, so firms would earn zero profits.

However, if firms can engage in informative advertising, there would be "Hotelling" competition. In this case, firms earn strictly positive profits. In conclusion, informative advertising can increase differentiation and reduce the intensity of price competition.

Suppose, on the other hand, that two firms sell homogeneous (identical) goods. Consumers are willing to pay v^3 for the good but are unaware of the firms' existence and price, so they must go through a search stage. If the consumer can only do one search, the equilibrium price is $p = v$. However, if firms can do informative advertising, the equilibrium price is $p = c$, where $c > v$. Consequently, informative advertising can increase the intensity of price competition.

Finally, Sutton's theory (1991) points out that in markets where differentiation is possible in the eyes of consumers, significant levels of advertising spending and a high degree of concentration will occur. In this case, advertising functions as a barrier to entry. For example, Borden's *RealLemon* brand dominated the US market for several years. The entry of a competitor, *Golden Crown*, with an identical product, triggered intensive advertising campaigns by *RealLemon* leading *Golden Crown* to set a price 15–25

3.3 To Remember

There are two types of advertising: informative advertising (providing information about the characteristics of the goods) and persuasive advertising (seeking to create subjective differentiation).

A monopoly sets its advertising expenditures such that the ratio of advertising expenditures to revenues equals the ratio of the elasticity of demand with respect to advertising to the elasticity of demand with respect to price.

Advertising on product features softens competition by increasing the opportunities for firms to differentiate.

Advertising on prices intensifies price competition.

3.4 Suggested Questions

1. A typical monopolistically competitive market is for:

[3] v is the consumer's willingness to pay.

   a. Flour.
   b. Public goods.
   c. Salt.
   d. Home appliances.

2. In monopolistic competition, there are:

   a. Many firms making a differentiated product.
   b. Few firms making a differentiated product.
   c. Many firms making an identical product.
   d. Few firms making an identical product.

3. Dole Co. operates in a monopolistically competitive market. Which of the following characterizes Dole Co.'s market?

   a. Dole Co. supplies a small portion of the market's output.
   b. Dole Co.'s product is slightly different from its competitors'.
   c. Dole Co. faced no barriers to entry when it decided to enter its market.
   d. All of the above describe the market for Dole Co.

4. Which of the following is not a characteristic of monopolistic competition?

   a. Many firms.
   b. Price-taking firms.
   c. Advertising.
   d. Product differentiation.

5. The key characteristic of monopolistic competition that distinguishes it from perfect competition is:

   a. Many sellers.
   b. Barriers to entry.
   c. Interdependence.
   d. Product differentiation.

6. Perfect competition and monopolistic competition are similar in that both market structures include:

   a. Price-taking behavior by firms.
   b. A homogeneous product.
   c. No barriers to entry.
   d. Very few firms.

7. The demand curve for each firm in monopolistic competition has:
    a. A slope of zero, and there are barriers to market entry.
    b. Negative slope, and there are no barriers to market entry.
    c. Negative slope, and there are barriers to market entry.
    d. A slope of zero, and there are no barriers to market entry.
8. Monopoly and monopolistic competition are different because:
    a. There is greater restriction on output in monopolistic competition.
    b. There are no barriers to entry in monopolistic competition.
    c. The marginal revenue and demand curves are the same for a monopoly.
    d. The slope of the demand curve that firms face.
9. In monopolistic competition:
    a. Firms do not have market power.
    b. Firms have market power, the ability to sell above marginal cost.
    c. The equilibrium of monopolistic competition is equal to the point of tangency between residual demand and the supply curve.
    d. Firms engage in strategic behavior because of the large number of competitors.
10. Suppose that firms compete by selling differentiated products but not perfect substitutes. Additionally, there is free entry and exit of firms. What market structure best describes the previous situation?
    a. Monopoly.
    b. Oligopoly.
    c. Monopolistic competition.
    d. Perfect competition.

CHAPTER 4

Oligopoly

4.1 Introduction

Within market structures, there is only one perfect competition model, only one model of monopoly, but several noncooperative oligopoly models. Consequently, oligopoly theory focuses on studying strategic interactions, using the concept of Nash equilibrium from game theory.

An oligopoly is an industry in which a small number of firms compete. Most markets that fit this description are telecommunications, computer software, mineral water, etc. In an oligopolistic market, a firm must carefully consider both the actions of its competitors and how they might react to its own decisions. Studying these strategic interactions is the purpose of oligopoly theory.

Producers of mineral water in France in 1993 are an example of this market type. Three companies (Danone, Nestlé, Castel) controlled 90% of this market (LSA Magazine 2008). These companies marketed different brands. For example, Danone owned Evian and Volvic; Nestlé owned Perrier and Contrex; and Castel marketed Saint-Yorre, Vichy, and Cristalline.

For this reason, the emergence of the Castel group is linked to a decision by the European Commission that allowed it to acquire mineral waters from the Vichy firm. In terms of health and well-being, the differentiation between mineral waters is primarily shaped by the packaging types, which

C. Lanchimba, *Industrial Organization*,
https://doi.org/10.1007/978-3-032-10906-4_4

complicates the price comparison. Despite this difficulty, we still analyze the interdependence of these companies' decisions. If a group increases the mineral water price, competitors can choose to do the same or not react to capture some customers.

The cellular telephone industry in Ecuador is another example of oligopoly. Three companies Conecel S.A. (Claro), Otecel (Movistar, Tuenti), and Corporación Nacional de Telecomunicaciones (CNT) control 100% of the market. Claro and Movistar control most of the market, so strategic decisions are interdependent. Thus, when Claro launches a 2 for 1 discount, Movistar does so as well.

Similarly, Medan and Warin (2000) point out that in the United States the market share of sugary soft drinks would be an oligopoly with Coca-Cola company with 44.5% of the market (in 200 countries), PepsiCo with 31.4% (leader in 40 countries), and Cadbury-Schweppes with 14.4%. By 2023, the United States had the highest per capita consumption of soft drinks, as reported by Orús (2024). According to Ridder (2024), the market share of sugary soft drinks in the United States was as follows: Coca-Cola Company at 46.3%, PepsiCo at 24.7%, and Keurig Dr Pepper at 14%. In total, Americans consumed 192 liters per person of sugary soft drinks within the country (Ridder 2024).

The three main models of noncooperative oligopoly with homogeneous goods are (i) the Cournot model, in which companies compete simultaneously in quantity; (ii) the Stackelberg model, which assumes that companies compete in quantity as in Cournot, but one of them has more information than the other; and (iii) Bertrand model, where companies compete in price.

These three models are the best-known and predate game theory. However, some authors consider them as game theory models. Furthermore, one-period models involve the concept of Nash equilibrium, i.e., all the strategies (or actions) that are optimal for each firm considering the actions of its competitors. In this way, no firm can obtain a higher profit (π) by choosing a different strategy. Additionally, we will study the Edgeworth model, whose competition involves price and cartels, which are a type of collusion between companies.

The basic structure of the oligopoly model is a quasi-competitive model, where a price-accepting behavior of all companies is assumed. The objective is to choose a production level that maximizes profits, considering how the other firm reacts to this production decision in which there is cost symmetry. Therefore, companies are identical, and their decisions affect the market price. The inverse demand function would be $p = f(Q) = f(q_1 + q_2 + \ldots + q_n)$, where $q_i (i = 1, \ldots, n)$ is the quantity produced by each firm. Therefore, each firm maximizes its profits individually as follows,

$$\pi_i = pq_i - c_i(q_i) \tag{4.1.1}$$

where π_i is the function that producer i wants to maximize, p is the market price, c_i is the production cost of firm i, and q_i is the quantity produced by firm i. Maximizing equation (4.1.1), we have

$$\frac{\delta \pi_i}{\delta q_i} = p - MC_i \Rightarrow p = MC_i. \tag{4.1.2}$$

Thus, the maximization functions of all firms together with the demand equation will cause the market to clear.

4.2 Models of Competition in Quantity

4.2.1 Cournot Model

The Cournot model, which was developed in 1838, studies the competition between the quantities produced by firms with identical weights. Each firm chooses the quantity that maximizes profit considering the existence of the other firm, that is, anticipating its behavior. This strategy does not seem natural for firms, since the strategic decision variable seems to be price. However, in sectors like agriculture or oil, firms cannot alter the price, though they do have the flexibility to choose the quantities they produce. The characteristics of noncooperative equilibrium can be summarized as follows:

- Each firm uses its competitor's output as a given, i.e., each firm anticipates that its competitor will maintain the output volume, regardless of how much it itself decides to produce. This scenario is the "null conjecture hypothesis." **This is a model of quantity competition, where the strategic decision variable of firms as its name indicates is quantity.**
- The market price is unique and there is a production equilibrium.
- Firms know the residual demand function, meaning each firm assumes that its competitors supply a fixed and unchanging quantity. As a

result, the firm calculates the residual demand—i.e., the portion of market demand not met by rivals—which it alone can satisfy. Within this segment, the firm behaves as a monopolist facing residual demand.

In a Cournot duopoly, we argue the market is a non-contestable duopoly, i.e., no new firms are entering. Furthermore, products are homogeneous, and the model is developed over a single period.

The variables that intervene in the model are the following: q_1, q_2 production level of firms 1 and 2, respectively. Therefore, $Q = q_1 + q_2$ is the total market demand. $\bar{q_1}$ *and* $\bar{q_2}$ are the hypothesized production level of firms 1 and 2 conjectured, respectively, by firms 2 and 1. c_1 and c_2 are the production costs of firms 1 and 2. Consequently, $MC_1(q_1)$ and $MC_2(q_2)$ represent the marginal costs of firms 1 and 2, and $\pi_1(q_1)$ and $\pi_2(q_2)$ are profits of firm 1 and 2, respectively. Finally, $p(q_1+q_2)$ represents the market price. Therefore, the maximization problem is given by Eq. (4.2.1) and (4.2.2).

$$\pi_{1\ (q_1,\bar{q_2})} = q_1 p(q_1, \bar{q_2}) - c_1(q_1) \tag{4.2.1}$$

and

$$\pi_{2\ (\bar{q_1},q_2)} = q_2 p(\bar{q_1}, q_2) - c_2(q_2). \tag{4.2.2}$$

The independent maximization conditions of the two profits are given by

$$\frac{\delta \pi_1}{\delta q_1} = p(q_1, \bar{q_2}) \frac{\delta p(q_1, \bar{q_2})}{\delta q_1} - \frac{\delta c_1(q_1)}{\delta q_1} = 0 \tag{4.2.3}$$

and

$$\frac{\delta \pi_2}{\delta q_2} = p(\bar{q_1}, q_2) \frac{\delta p(\bar{q_1}, q_2)}{\delta q_2} - \frac{\delta c_2(q_2)}{\delta q_2} = 0. \tag{4.2.4}$$

The equilibrium satisfies the two first-order conditions. These two equations can be considered as implicit functions. Equation (4.2.3) defines q_1 in terms of q_2, that is, the best response of firm 1 to the decisions of firm 2. Thus, the reaction function of firm 1 is $q_1^* = R1(\bar{q_2})$. Equation (4.2.4) defines the reaction function of firm 2 $q_2^* = R2(\bar{q_1})$. These two functions are decreasing, a firm expects its competitors' output to rise, but its optimal output is low. The independent profit maximization conditions of the two profits are given by the Eq. (4.2.5) and (4.2.6):

$$p(q_1 + \bar{q_2}) + q_1 \frac{\delta p}{\delta Q} - MC_1(q_1) = 0 \tag{4.2.5}$$

and

$$p(\bar{q_1} + q_2) + q_2 \frac{\delta p}{\delta Q} - MC_2(q_2) = 0 \tag{4.2.6}$$

We are working with a derivative of the form $\frac{\delta p}{\delta Q}$ rather than the partial derivatives $\frac{\delta p}{\delta q_1}$ or $\frac{\delta p}{\delta q_2}$. This is because we made the null hypothesis conjecture, meaning that when firm 1 changes its output q_1, it believes that firm 2's output q_2 remains unchanged As a result; any change in total quantity $Q(q1 + q2)$ results from the firm's own decision.

In Cournot equilibrium, each firm sells the quantity that maximizes its profit, given its expectation of the quantity produced by another firm. The equilibrium condition assumes these expectations are correct; each firm's forecast about its rival's output is confirmed in equilibrium. However, producers' guesses are usually wrong[1] because his competitor modifies his production in response to changes in a rival's output. However, it is possible to define a situation where the guesses are correct in the *Cournot equilibrium*. The Cournot equilibrium is a set of production decisions (q_1^*, q_2^*) such that $q_1^* = R_1(q_2^*)$ and $q_2^* = R_2(q_1^*)$. In this equilibrium, guesses disappear altogether (intersection of the two reaction curves).

In equilibrium, no firm wants to change its choice. The Cournot equilibrium is a special case of the Nash equilibrium. The *Cournot-Nash equilibrium* is anachronistic because the Nash equilibrium is from 1950 and the Cournot model from 1838. There are two ways to interpret equilibrium determination: *(i) Simultaneous*: firms simultaneously choose their production because their decision predicts that of their competitor. Equilibrium is reached when expectations coincide with the decisions taken. *(ii) Result of a process:* each firm alternately modifies its production volume taking into account the previous decision of its competitor, until equilibrium is reached.

In a one-period model, for example, firms choose their production independently of each other. This Cournot equilibrium is the most realistic and the most plausible.

[1] An agent is said to make Cournot guesses if he considers the actions of others as given, without considering that those actions may be influenced by his actions.

Example

1. Suppose two firms are competing in Cournot competition, with output levels q_1, q_2 for firms 1 and 2, respectively. The quantity available in the market is $Q = q_1 + q_2$. Moreover, $\bar{q_1}, \bar{q_2}$ are the output levels of firms 1 and 2 as guessed by 2 and 1, respectively. C_1, C_2 are the production costs of firms 1 and 2, and $\pi_1(q_1), \pi_2(q_2)$ are the profits of each firm, respectively.

   On the other hand, the inverse demand function is $p = 60 - Q$. The costs are $C_1 = (q_1)^2$ for firm 1 and $C_2 = 15q_2 + (q_2)^2$ for firm 2. For this analysis, it is necessary to determine the situation of companies 1 and 2 separately, thus obtaining the reaction function for each of them. Obtaining the reaction function means that we are going to find the optimal quantities for q_1, which will be a function of $\bar{q_2}$ and vice versa for the optimal quantity of q_2. Subsequently, the system of equations is solved to determine the equilibrium quantities, and the corresponding profits for each firm are then calculated. We will start with company 1 which makes a guess about firm 2's output ($\bar{q_2}$). The equilibrium for this company would be

$$\pi_1 = q_1(60 - q_1 - \bar{q_2}) - (q_1)^2$$

$$\frac{\delta \pi_1}{\delta q_1} = 60 - 2q_1 - \bar{q_2} - 2q_1 = 0.$$

   Therefore, $q_1^* = 15 - \frac{1}{4}\bar{q_2} = R_1(\bar{q_2})$ is firm 1's best response to $\bar{q_2}$. Firm 1's reaction curve can be represented graphically (Fig. 4.1).

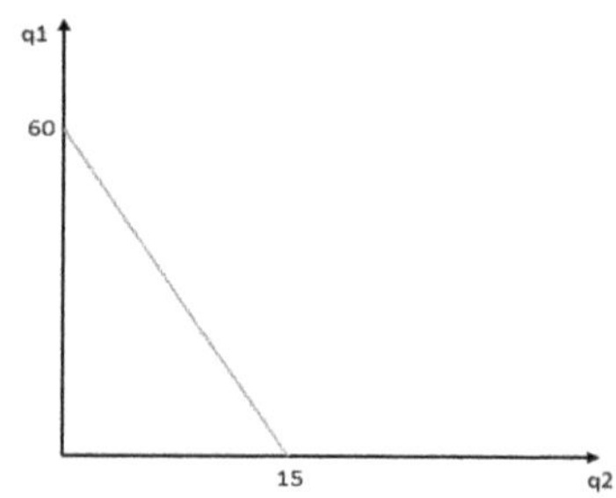

Fig. 4.1
Representation of firm 1.
Source: Author

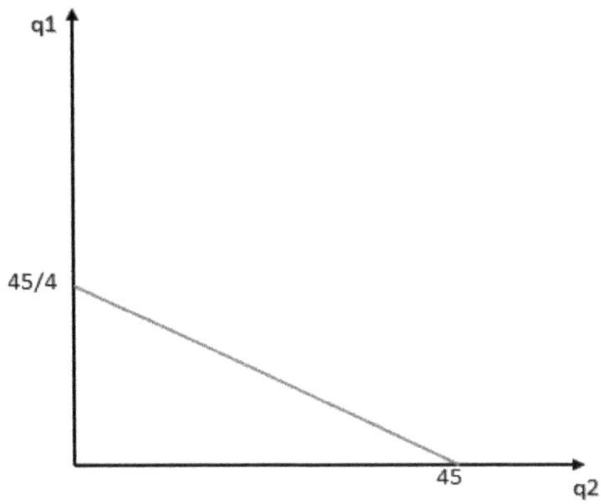

Fig. 4.2
Representation of firm 2.
Source: Author

The equilibrium for firm 2 (with $\bar{q_1}$) will be

$$\pi_2 = q_2(60 - q_1 - q_2) - 15q_2 - (q_2)^2$$

$$\frac{\delta\pi_2}{\delta q_2} = 60 - q_1 - 2q_2 - 15 - 2q_2 = 0.$$

$q_2^* = \frac{45-\bar{q_1}}{4} = R_2(\bar{q_1})$ is the best response of firm 2 to $\bar{q_1}$. Similarly, firm 2's reaction curve can be represented in Fig. 4.2.

An equilibrium is reached when each firm's output level is the best response to the other firm's output level. In this sense, neither firm has an incentive to deviate from its output level. Thus, a pair of output levels (q_1^*, q_2^*) is a Cournot-Nash equilibrium if the following condition occurs: $q1^* = R1(\bar{q2})$ and $q2^* = R2(\bar{q1})$. Therefore, the system of equations must be solved to find the values of q_1^* and q_2^*:

$$q_1^* = R_1(q_2^*) = 15 - \frac{1}{4}q_2^*$$

and

$$q_2^* = R_1(q_1^*) = \frac{45 - q_1^*}{4}$$

Substituting q_2^*, we have

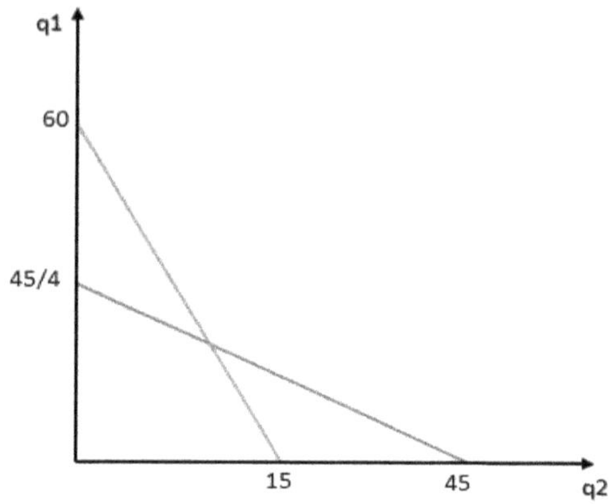

Fig. 4.3 Cournot equilibrium. Source: Author

$$q_1^* = 15 - \frac{1}{4}\left(\frac{45 - q1^*}{4}\right) \Rightarrow q_1^* = 13$$

whence

$$q_2^* = \frac{45 - 13}{4} = 8.$$

These values represent the Cournot-Nash equilibrium, which is the point of intersection between the reaction curves of firm 1 and 2 (Fig. 4.3).

2. Consider two firms ($i = 1, 2$) that produce the same good and that choose their level of production independently ($q_i \epsilon \mathbb{R}^+$). Suppose that the inverse demand function is

$$p(q) = \begin{cases} \alpha - (q_1 + q_2) & , si\ q_1 + q_2 \leq \alpha \\ 0 & , si\ q_1 + q_2 > \alpha \end{cases} \tag{4.2.7}$$

where $q = (q_1, q_2)$ is the output of firm 1 and 2, respectively, and p is the price. Both firms have a total cost of $C_1 = \frac{1}{2}q_1^2$ and $C_2 = q_2$.

Each firm maximizes its profits π_i:

$$\begin{aligned} \pi_1(q_1, \bar{q_2}) =& (\alpha - (q_1 + \bar{q_2}))q_1 - \frac{1}{2}q_1^2 \\ \pi_2(\bar{q_1}, q_2) =& (\alpha - (\bar{q_1} + q_2))q_2 - q_2 \end{aligned} \tag{4.2.8}$$

The profit of firm i is presented in Eq. (4.2.9):

$$\begin{aligned}\frac{\delta\pi_1}{\delta q_1} &= \alpha - 3q_1 - q_2 \\ \frac{\delta\pi_2}{\delta q_2} &= \alpha - q_1 - 2q_2 - 1.\end{aligned} \tag{4.2.9}$$

Therefore, the equilibrium (Cournot-Nash) is given by Eq. (4.2.10):

$$\left(q_1^* = \frac{\alpha+1}{5}, q_2^* = \frac{2\alpha-3}{5}\right), \tag{4.2.10}$$

and the equilibrium price is presented in Eq. (4.2.11):

$$p^* = \frac{2\alpha+2}{5}. \tag{4.2.11}$$

Finally, the profits are in Eq. (4.2.12):

$$\begin{aligned}\pi_1(q_1, q_2) &= \frac{3}{2}\left(\frac{\alpha+1}{5}\right)^2 \\ \pi_2(q_1, q_2) &= \left(\frac{2\alpha-3}{5}\right)^2.\end{aligned} \tag{4.2.12}$$

Market's profit is in Eq. (4.2.13):

$$\pi(q_1, q_2) = \frac{11\alpha^2 - 18\alpha + 21}{50}. \tag{4.2.13}$$

If $\alpha = 100$, the market profits are 2164.42, when $Q^* = q_1 + q_2 = 20.2 + 39.4 = 59.6$, and $p^* = 40.4$, where the profits are 612.06 and 1552.36, for firms 1 and 2, respectively.

4.2.1.1 Remarks on Cournot Equilibrium

1. *Cournot equilibrium and social optimum:* The social optimum is defined by the equality of price and marginal cost (as in competitive

equilibrium). However, the Cournot equilibrium lies between the perfect competition equilibrium and the monopoly equilibrium.

2. *Cournot oligopoly with three or more firms:* When there are more than two identical firms in the market, Cournot equilibrium is determined by applying the same analysis. In this case, the optimal response function of firm 1 is: $q_1 = R_1(q_1, \ldots, q_n)$. Finally, the higher the number of firms, the higher the output and the lower the prices per firm, but the firms' output of the firms increases.

4.2.2 Stackelberg Model

This is a noncooperative oligopoly competition model dating back to 1934, where the quantity is the strategic decision variable. In this model, there is information asymmetry between companies since they do not have the same market power. Some have a finer perception of their competitors' strategies. This structure is similar to Cournot's model, where firms choose the quantities; they will supply to the market. However, in this version, one firm can anticipate how its competitors will react to its decisions.

In the Cournot model, the company assumes that the other companies do not react. On the contrary, in the Stackelberg model, the entrepreneur integrates information about the decisions of the other companies into its process to maximize its profits. The leader, the better-informed company in the market, knows the reaction function of the other companies, so it can attract more profits in the market. The other firms are known as followers, which are firms that act in the "Cournot" mode.

Building on the Cournot model, the profit equations are reformulated by replacing firm 1's conjecture $\bar{q_2}$ by the reaction function $q_1 = R_1(\bar{q_2})$. Then, the profits of the leading firm (1) are

$$\pi_1 = q_1 p(q_1 + R_1(q_2)) - C_1. \tag{4.2.14}$$

Equation (4.2.14) refers to the firm 1's profits. This equation no longer contains the variable $\bar{q_2}$, which implies the leader does not guess about the follower but already has the reaction function (it has more information). In other words, firm 1 knows how firm 2 behaves. Therefore, it chooses its production level, knowing in advance all the consequences of its decisions.

On the other hand, the profits of the follower firm are

$$\pi_2 = q_2 p(\overline{q_1} + q_2) - C_2 \tag{4.2.15}$$

where the Eq. (4.2.15) refers to firm 2's profit. This equation contains the variable $\bar{q_1}$, which implies firm 2 guesses about firm 1's behavior because it has less information. In other words, firm 2 behaves as in the Cournot model.

Finally, the solution to this game is a Nash equilibrium. The Stackelberg equilibrium allows the *leader* (firm 1) to achieve a higher profit due to its better perception of the market.

Example Consider the same situation as above where two firms ($i = 1, 2$) independently choose their level of output while producing the same good ($q_i \epsilon \mathbb{R}^+$).The reaction function of Firm 2 is given by $q_2^* = \frac{\alpha-1-q_1}{2}$.

This function describes Firm 2's optimal response for any given q_1, that is, the quantity q_2 that Firm 2 will choose. Firm 1, assuming Firm 2 is rational and aware of its own production environment, can anticipate Firm 2's decision through its known reaction function. Thus, when firm 1 maximizes its profits (Eq. 4.2.16), it takes into account that Firm 2's quantity is determined by the previously established reaction function:

$$\pi_1(q_1) = \left(\alpha - q_1 - \frac{\alpha - 1 - q_1}{2}\right) q_1 - \frac{1}{2} q_1^2 \tag{4.2.16}$$

The profits for firm 1 are:

$$\frac{\delta \pi_1(q_1)}{\delta q1} = \frac{\alpha + 1}{2} - 2q_1.$$

Therefore, $q_1^* = \frac{\alpha+1}{4}$.

Replacing q_1 by q_2 , we have $q_2^* = \frac{3\alpha-5}{8}$, and the price is $p^* = \frac{3}{8}(\alpha + 1)$.

The profits of firm 1 are given by $\pi_1(q_1, q_2) = \frac{(\alpha+1)^2}{16}$, while the profits of firm 2 are $\pi_2(q_2, q_1) = (\frac{3\alpha-5}{8})^2$. Therefore, the market profits are $\pi(q_1, q_2) = \frac{13\alpha^2-22\alpha+29}{64}$.

If $\alpha = 100$, $Q = q_2 + q_1 = 25.25 + 36.875 = 62.125$, the market price is 37.875, and the profits of firms 1 and 2 are 637.56 and 1359.77, respectively. Therefore, the market profits are 1997.33.

Compared to the results of the Cournot model, the profits of Firm 2 decreased, while those of Firm 1 increased. Therefore, the leader can know how firm 2 reacts, which allows him to adjust his strategy (by volume) to maximize his own profit, achieving higher profits than in the previous equilibrium. However, it does not mean that Firm 1 will have the highest profits because they depend on the marginal cost of each firm.

4.3 Price Competition Models

4.3.1 Bertrand Model

This noncooperative oligopoly model dates to 1883 when Bertrand disagreed with the idea that the firm's decision variable is quantity. Bertrand formulated a more realistic hypothesis, where the decision variable is price. The assumptions of the model are the following: (i) firms compete on price; (ii) products are homogenous (or perfect substitutes), at least in the eyes of consumers; (iii) firms have no restrictions on production capacity; and (iv) firms behave symmetrically, i.e., they have the same information. Therefore, firms are aware of all competitors' prices, and consumers are fully informed, purchasing only from the firm that offers the lowest price.

The Nash equilibrium resulting from this game is a pair of prices such that each price maximizes profits given the choice made by the other firm. Suppose two firms i and j propose prices p_i and p_j, respectively, where the cost is constant and identical and equals to $C_i = cq_i$ for the two firms. Furthermore, the demand has the form presented in the Eq. (4.3.1):

$$q(p) = \begin{cases} \alpha - p & , si\ p\ \varepsilon\ [0, \alpha] \\ 0 & , si\ p > \alpha \end{cases} \tag{4.3.1}$$

In this context, if firms set the same price, they split the market demand equally. The demand function for firm i is

$$d_i(p_i, p_j) = \begin{cases} \alpha - p_i\ si,\ p_i < p_j \\ \frac{\alpha - p_i}{2}\ si,\ p_i = p_j. \\ 0\ si,\ p_i > p_j \end{cases} \tag{4.3.2}$$

Given that each firm considers its competitor' price as given, it has an incentive to slightly undercut that price to capture the entire market. The demand function (4.3.2) has three different possible cases for i: (i) if $p_i < p_j$, firm i captures all the demand; (ii) $\frac{1}{2}D_i(p_i)$ if $p_i = p_j$; in this case, firms i and j split the demand equally, (iii) if $p_i > p_j$, firm i has no demand. In this context, the profit function of firm i is:

$$\pi_i(p_i, p_j) = \begin{cases} (p_i - c)(\alpha - p_i)\ si,\ p_i < p_j \\ \frac{(p_i - c)(\alpha - p_i)}{2}\ si,\ p_i = p_j \\ 0\ si,\ p_i > p_j. \end{cases} \quad (4.3.3)$$

To determine the equilibrium, suppose that $min \quad p_i, p_j < \alpha$. As a result, the demand is always positive, and four equilibria are possible:

1. Suppose that $min \quad p_i, p_j < c$. In this case, if $p_i < p_j$ and $p_i < c$, the profit of firm 1 is negative, and the firm is not interested in producing at this price. Therefore, it cannot be the Nash equilibrium.
2. Suppose that $p_i > p_j > c$. In that case, firm j obtains the market demand and a positive profit, and firm i obtains zero profits.

   For example, if firm i decides to set a lower price than firm j, $p_i^1 = p_j - a$ (where a is a positive constant), and firm i will obtain all the demand,

$$\begin{aligned} \pi &= (p_i - a - c)(\alpha - p_i + a) \quad (4.3.4) \\ \pi &= (p_i - c)(\alpha - p_i) + a(2p_i - \alpha - a - c - \alpha) \\ \pi &= \bar{\pi}_i^1 + a(2p_i - \alpha - a - c - \alpha) > 0 \end{aligned}$$

   for a close to 0 since $\bar{\pi}_i^1 > 0$. Therefore, firm i has an incentive to lower its price when $p_i > p_j > c$, meaning this situation is not a Nash equilibrium.
3. Suppose that $p_i = p_j > c$. In this case, firm 1 has an incentive to set a price $p_i^1 = p_j - a$ since it will obtain:

$$\begin{aligned} (p_j - a - c)(\alpha - p_i + a) &= \quad (4.3.5) \\ (p_i - c)(\alpha - p_j) + a(2p_i - \alpha - c - a) &> \frac{(p_i - c)(\alpha - p_i)}{2} \end{aligned}$$

   for a close enough to 0. Therefore, this is not a Nash equilibrium either.

   Points 3 and 4 can be summarized as follows: if firm j lowers its price slightly, holding all other things equal, it can capture the entire market demand. Similarly, if firm i always has an incentive to slightly undercut Firm $j's$ price, j can reason the same way. As a result, any

price above marginal cost cannot be a Nash equilibrium for either firm.
4. Suppose that $p_i = p_j = p = c$. In this case, no firm has an interest in changing the price.

In this case, there exists a unique Nash equilibrium such that firms set $p_i^* = p_j^* = MC$, i.e., $\pi_i^* = \pi_j^* = 0$. As a result, we have a "paradox," because by changing from one firm (monopoly) to two firms (duopoly), the equilibrium price changes from the monopoly price to the perfect competition price. In other words, two firms are enough to achieve a perfect competition equilibrium. This situation, which seems unreal, is known as the *Bertrand paradox*.

Therefore, in the Bertrand equilibrium, the firms obtain zero profits. The equilibrium price corresponds to the social optimum $p = MC$ (see Chap. 2). In this context, a common approach to resolving the Bertrand paradox, i.e., explaining why prices may exceed marginal cost, is to relax the assumption of product homogeneity. However, we could assume collusion. If both firms sell at a price above the marginal cost, they could even set a monopoly price $p_i = p_j = p_m$ to obtain positive profits. Another possible resolution involves tacit collusion between i and j , which can arise through repeated interaction in the framework of the iterated prisoner's dilemma. Another solution is for firms to have limited production capacity, which is known as the *Edgeworth model*.

A real-world example of the Bertrand model is the 2006 price war between the chip manufacturers Intel and AMD. AMD ended the year with losses, and Intel reduced its profit by 42% in the year. In an interview, Mario Rivas (CEO of AMD, source: la expansion), stated: *This price war with Intel is ridiculous (...). The problem is that despite its 2 billion dollars of reserves, Intel has 7 plants to run at full speed. They lower the price, and we have no choice but to follow them.*

4.3.1.1 *Edgeworth Model*

This model deals with price competition under capacity constraints, where i offers the lowest prices ($p_i = MC$), but cannot cover the entire demand. As a result, there is a residual demand directed to j since $p_j > MC$: j earns a positive profit. Capacity constraints offer a solution to the price competition by preventing prices from falling to marginal cost. However, no equilibrium is stable.

Consider a small seaside town with two hotels and a fixed number of rooms; in other words, the firms face capacity constraints in their production. If one hotel charges a higher room price, customers will choose its competitor. However, once the lower-priced hotel reaches full capacity, some customers will have to stay at the more expensive hotel. Therefore, this hotel will make a profit and end up lowering its prices. In response, the other hotel does the same. As a result, the price war ensues until the average cost reaches its minimum and firm makes zero profits. However, this situation is not stable as one of the hotels will eventually increase its prices. This hotel will lose a share of the demand, but it will still make a profit, unlike its competitor. The competitor will eventually increase its prices, leading to a general increase in hotel rooms prices.

This cycle will be reversed when demand is zero, and the subsequent price-cutting phase ends when profits reach zero. To sum up, Edgeworth model does not yield a stable equilibrium.

4.4 Collusion

We speak of collusion, cartel, or collusive practice when companies agree to operate in a market at the expense of their clients or suppliers, to have profits higher than the "normal" ones they would have if they competed. The "normal" profits are those of the noncooperative Nash equilibrium (Bertrand, Cournot, Stackelbert). For example, companies can agree on prices or the division of the market. Collusion can be of two general types: explicit, where companies agree explicitly on prices as well as other strategic variables such as output levels, production capacity, investments in research and development, and tacit, where firms coordinate their behavior to sustain profits above the competitive level without any formal agreement.

One of the most well-known cartels in the world is the Organization of the Petroleum Exporting Countries (OPEC). Its primary objective is to coordinate production levels among member countries, as the price of oil is largely determined by the total quantity supplied to the market. This quantity must guarantee the maximum profit possible for its members. In addition, the cartel decides on the allocation of the quantity produced among its members. In other words, the cartel deals with the allocation of production quotas among its members.

The cartel is viable when its members respect the agreements reached. These incentives will depend, among other things, on the observability of the behavior of each member and the existence of sanctions in case of violation of the commitment. One of OPEC's key challenges is ensuring that members do not exceed their assigned production quotas, thereby acting as "free riders." If all members exceed their quotas, world oil production is much higher than expected, oil prices are much lower, and, finally, each OPEC member is in a less favorable situation than if all cartel members had complied with the agreement.

In this context, one of the main reasons cartels emerge is that firms in a market have incentives to collude and increase their market power and boost their profits. On the other hand, in a competitive economy, firms are supposed to "maximize their profits." Why then form a cartel that limits its output levels? This behavior arises because competitive markets can resemble a prisoner's dilemma: each firm independently sets its strategy (by setting prices, quantities, and investments) to maximize profits, without accounting for the impact on competitors. In contrast, a cartel allows firms to coordinate and internalize the effects of their decisions on one another's profits.

In summary, firms may reach agreements or collude on three main aspects: (i) setting a common price, (ii) jointly determining output levels (though this is less common), and (iii) dividing markets geographically. However, similar behaviors can exist in markets without collusion. Some concerted behavior is allowed under certain conditions.

Example Firms agree to choose an output level q_1, q_2. Suppose the inverse demand function is

$$p(q) = \begin{cases} \alpha - (q_1 + q_2) & , si\ q \leq \alpha \\ 0 & , si\ q > \alpha \end{cases}$$

where p is the price. Firm 1 has a total cost $c_1 = \frac{1}{2}q_1^2$ and firm 2 has a total cost of $c_2 = q_2$. Each firm chooses $i \epsilon 1, 2$ and chooses the quantity that maximizes its profits π_i:

$$\pi(q_1, q_2) = \pi_1(q_1, q_2) + \pi_2(q_1, q_2)$$

$$\pi(q_1, q_2) = (\alpha - (q_1 + q_2))q_1 - \frac{1}{2}q_1^2 + (\alpha - (q_1 + q_2))q_2 - q_2$$

The firms behave like a monopoly with two branches. The profits of the firm are as follows:

$$\frac{\delta\pi(q_1, q_2)}{\delta q_1} = \alpha - 3q_1 - 2q_2$$
$$\frac{\delta\pi(q_1, q_2)}{\delta q_1} = \alpha - 1 - 2q_1 - 2q_2$$

Therefore,

$$q_1 = \frac{\alpha - 2q_2}{3}$$
$$q_2 = \frac{\alpha - 1 - 2q_1}{2}.$$

Solving the system of equations $q_1^* = 1$, $q_2^* = \frac{\alpha-3}{2}$, $p^* = \frac{\alpha+1}{2}$. Consequently, the profits are

$$\pi_1(q_1, q_2) = \frac{\alpha}{2}$$
$$\pi_2(q_1, q_2) = \frac{\alpha^2 - 4\alpha + 3}{4}$$
$$\pi(q_1, q_2) = \frac{\alpha^2 - 2\alpha + 3}{4}.$$

Thus, the cartel operates as a monopoly with two production plants. Assuming $\alpha = 100$, $Q = q_1 + q_2 = 1 + 48.5 = 49.5$, $p = 50.5$, the profits of firm 1 and 2 are 50 and 2400.75, respectively, so the market profits are 2450.75. Consequently, firm 1's profit is lower under the cartel (50) than under Cournot competition (612). As a result, firm 1 is reluctant to form the cartel. The most profitable market structure is a monopoly, as the monopolist can maximize joint profits by internalizing all production decisions. In fact, monopoly profits typically exceed those achieved under a collusive arrangement, since total production costs are together, and competition is eliminated. In Chap. 2, the monopolist's profits with cost $c = \frac{3q}{2}$ and $p = \alpha - q$ add up to $\pi^* = \frac{(2\alpha-3)^2}{16}$. If $\alpha = 100$, the monopolist earns 2425.56, effectively capturing the entire surplus in the economy.

4.4.1 Cartels in the Real World

Although sectors such as transportation, telecommunications, and banks have strong incentives to collude and relax competition, many obstacles make it difficult to generalize this structure. The main limitation is that *collusion is usually prohibited* by competition policy. However, this is not enough to discourage the formation of cartels.

The most prominent example of a cartel is the Organization of the Petroleum Exporting Countries (OPEC). However, there is disagreement about whether it has cartel power. Kisswani (2011) notes that over the past four decades, models have been developed to examine OPEC's behavior and ability to influence oil prices. Yet, the question of whether OPEC truly functions as a cartel remains a subject of ongoing debate. Despite this, standard economics textbooks frequently present OPEC as a textbook example of a profit-maximizing cartel—one that sets production quotas, allocates market shares, and seeks to stabilize or elevate prices. Kisswani's review of the literature highlights this controversy, arguing the lack of conclusive evidence on OPEC's production behavior as a cartel.

Another well-known example of cartels is the Gas Exporting Countries Forum (GECF), which was founded in 2001 to maximize the value of natural gas by promoting it as a fuel and thus positioning the GECF as an internationally registered organization. It should be noted that some of the main exporters and producers are not members of the GECF, such as the United States and Australia. In contrast to OPEC, the GECF has consistently denied any intention to coordinate or set natural gas prices (Congressional Research Service 2018). Furthermore, it has not imposed production quotas on member states, and its charter has no authority to introduce such quotas.

On the other hand, companies in a cartel share a common interest in reducing competition through collaboration. However, each firm also has strong incentives to "cheat" or "deviate" from the cooperative equilibrium (opportunistic behavior) to increase its profits. A firm, for instance, can lower its prices to capture a larger market share, and other firms may follow as a response. This internal instability makes collusion impossible and is a key vulnerability of cartels. It stems from the fact that cartels are illegal in many jurisdictions and thus cannot enforce contracts or agreements among its members.

Punishment mechanisms are therefore needed to deter "cheats." These mechanisms are self-enforcing, meaning that firms adhere to them voluntarily. They include mutual threats of future retaliation such as price wars, sabotage, or even physical retaliation.

Cartels and collusion are socially inefficient since there is a welfare loss when the price rises above marginal cost: "deadweight loss" (social welfare criterion, i.e., price equals marginal cost). There is also a transfer from consumers to producers (consumer surplus criterion). However, Taylor (2002), in his analysis of manufacturing sector cartels formed under the National Industrial Recovery Act of 1933 in the United States, argues that such cartels could be socially beneficial. Contrary to conventional expectations, he finds that these cartels were associated with higher levels of production. This result is because cartels, through coordination between their members, can better deal with problems related to costs and, therefore, be more efficient. However, the empirical evidence presented in the study does not support this theoretical prediction. In fact, in the period analyzed, government-sponsored cartels reduced production in the sector, which is in line with the traditional literature on cartels.

4.4.1.1 Collusion: Interactions and Punishments

Collusion requires repeated interactions and a sanction mechanism, either tacit or explicit. There is a "punishment" for the cheater in case of deviation from the collusive equilibrium. The "punishment" can be a temporary price war, i.e., actions to reduce the company's profit that has deviated. This "punishment" must be sufficiently expensive compared to the profits related to a "deviation." It must also be relatively inexpensive for the firms enforcing it. In this sense, for the threat of punishment to be effective, any deviation must be observable, ensuring that firms can detect and respond to noncompliant behavior.

An example of punishment in a cartel can be observed in the diamond market, where the De Beers company, founded in 1870, dominates the world market. De Beers controls the Central Sales Organization (CSO) of diamonds, which is responsible for the marketing and distribution of diamonds. At its peak, more than 80% of world production passed through CSOs. Producers are interested in using the services of CSOs because of their market expertise, strong advertising campaigns, price stabilization mechanisms, and the implicit threat of retaliation in the event of deviation from the agreement. A notable example occurred in 1981 when Zaire tried to deviate from the agreements reached. Two months later, a large quantity of unidentified diamonds came to the market, which dropped prices by almost 40%. This event was widely interpreted as a sanction against Zaire.

4.4.2 A Model of Collusion

Let us assume that two firms selling identical products (perfect substitutes) with identical marginal costs, c, operating under the assumptions of Bertrand competition. However, we consider a repeated game of finite horizon. At each instant $t = 0, 1, \ldots, \infty$, the two firms establish prices simultaneously, conditional on the previously fixed prices. We observe p^m, the monopoly price, and π^m, the monopoly profit. In addition, we verify that δ is the discount factor.[2]

An investor could invest 1 today to receive \$1 $+ r$ next period, where r is the interest rate per period. This relationship can be expressed as follows:

$$\delta = \frac{1}{1 + r}$$

Applying a discount factor to future benefits converts them into their present value. This concept is fundamental in project evaluation, where the Net Present Value (NPV) is commonly calculated to assess the profitability of an investment

$$VAN = \Sigma_{t=1}^{n} \frac{V_t}{(1 + k)^t} - I_o$$

where V_t represents the cash flows in each period t, I_0 is the value of the initial investment outlay, n is the number of periods considered, and k is the interest rate.

In this context, the following strategy is considered: in the *collusion period*, one firm sets the price $p = p^m$ (monopoly price) if the other firm sets p^m in the preceding periods. Subsequently, in the *punishment period*, one firm sets $p = c$ after a deviation (i.e., if the other firm sets a price $p < p^m$ in the preceding period).

Thus, we determine that tacit collusion is sustainable when the benefits of continued cooperation outweigh the short-term gains from deviation.

[2] Value of a dollar today that will be earned in the next period, generally $\delta < 1$.

In each period, each firm sets the monopoly price. Thus, in each period, both firms share the monopoly profits. The present profit in the case of continued collusion is:

$$\Pi = \frac{1}{2}\pi^m + \delta\frac{1}{2}\pi^m + \delta^2\frac{1}{2}\pi^m + \ldots = \frac{1}{2}\pi^m(1 + \delta + \delta^2 + \ldots); \qquad (4.4.1)$$

the producer seeks the inducement to deviate from the collusion agreement, which is the net gain in case of deviation. This gain would be:

$$\bar{\pi} = \pi^m + \delta^0 + \ldots = \pi^m. \qquad (4.4.2)$$

The producer must compare the payoffs between (4.4.1) and (4.4.2). At any time, the best deviation is to set a price equal to $p^m - \epsilon$. No firm has an interest in deviating if its payoff in case of deviation is less than its payoff in case of collusion if $\bar{\pi} < \pi^m$ (π^m monopoly profit).

Collusion is therefore sustainable if, for each firm, the long-term cost of retaliation exceeds the short-term gain from deviating from the agreement. In other words, firms must place a sufficiently high value on future profits for the threat of punishment to effectively deter deviation. Cartel instability can also come from outside through the entry of new firms attracted by profits. If new firms do not join the cartel, this can destabilize the entire structure as these new entrants can offer cheaper prices than the cartel members. Therefore, the cartel incentives to introduce strong barriers to entry.

4.4.2.1 Collusion and Barriers to Entry

Collusion is difficult to sustain if there are low barriers to entry since competitive entry reduces the gains from collusion (e.g., "*hit-and-run*" entry type). Additionally, there is the possibility of entry by competing firms in the future which would reduce the "threat" of "punishment" in case of deviation.

Suppose that in each period there is a probability μ of entry by a competitive firm that would set the competitive price $p = c$. With probability $1-\mu$, no entry occurs, and the two incumbent firms can sustain collusion. The two firms set the monopoly price in case of collusion and $p = c$ in case of deviation from the other firm in the market.

There is a direct relationship between barriers to entry and the sustainability of collusion as the threat of new competition undermines the stability of cooperative agreements. Therefore, a higher probability of entry (lower barriers to entry) reduces the gains from collusion. Thus, the benefits of future collusion reduce the "cost" of deviation (punishment).

4.4.2.2 *Secret Price Cut*

An example of collusion and punishment, borrowing from the Green and Porter (1984) model, assumes that in a market with two firms each firm observes its price and sales, but not its rival's price and sales, with probability α. Thus, demand disappears, i.e., it becomes equal to 0, after an "exogenous shock." This scenario arises because, when a firm faces zero demand, it cannot distinguish whether the cause is a negative demand shock or a deviation by its rival from the collusive agreement. In this context, perfect collusion is not viable, i.e., the possibility of charging monopoly prices even after a demand shock. However, collusion is always possible by implementing the following strategy:

- **Collusion phase**: It starts by setting the monopoly price and maintaining it as long as each firm keeps its market share.
- **Punishment phase**: When a firm's demand is zero, it triggers a price war that lasts for a finite number of periods (T), after which they return to the monopoly price p^m.

There is arbitrary in the choice of *T*, since the price war should be enough to deter "cheaters." However, a price war may have been triggered by a bad demand shock, not a "deviation." Firms have an incentive to limit the duration of the price war.

In conclusion, if price reductions are difficult to observe, periodic price wars may be necessary to operate a cartel. Even though there are periods of price wars in equilibrium in this model, no firm cheats in equilibrium.

On the other hand, if demand fluctuations are observable, demand is cyclical (up and down), and demand shocks are independent from period to period, the gains in collusion do not depend on the level of demand due to the assumption of independence. However, the gains in case of deviation depend on the level of demand if the deviation is most profitable and demand is high. Then, prices move in a "counter-cyclical" manner.

However, some clauses facilitate collusion. For example, one type of clause is "If you find the product cheaper, we will refund you the difference…." This clause facilitates the identification of deviations. Another clause is the "most favored customer clause" which affects the incentives for deviation. If the firm reduces its price to capture short-term demand, it must refund its previous customers who had paid the monopoly price. Therefore, this type of clause greatly reduces the incentives for deviation significantly and turns them into more stable cartels.

Another example of collusion and punishment occurred between 2008 and 2010 in the UK banking sector. During this period, RBS and Barclays engaged in explicit collusion in the market for bank loans, particularly targeting professionals such as lawyers and accountants. The two banks coordinated on pricing, maintaining artificially high loan rates through price agreements. The Office of Fair Trading (OFT) found them guilty, and RBS was fined £28.59 million (Pettinger 2020).

Finally, other factors that promote collusion are cost asymmetries, which make collusion difficult for two reasons: (i) it is difficult to reach agreement on a common pricing strategy, and (ii) it is difficult to "discipline" the most efficient firms. Furthermore, when a market is growing, collusion is easier to withstand since the gain from deviation is low compared to the cost of production.

4.5 To Remember

The models presented in this section can be summarized as follow (see Table 4.1):

It can be argued that the most accurate model depends on the flexibility of production capacity in other words, on whether firms can easily adjust their output or not. Thus, Bertrand competition is a better representation of oligopoly competition. Otherwise, if the capacity is more rigid, the Cournot competition model is more appropriate.

Markets with rigid capacity, such as those for physical goods like cars or airplanes, typically face greater constraints in adjusting output. In contrast, markets for services—such as banking or insurance—generally allow for more flexible capacity adjustments. For example, consider a change in music distribution, from the sale of physical

Table 4.1 Oligopoly models. Source: Author

Quantity competition	Price competition
The Cournot model (firm symmetry)	The Bertrand model (without capacity restriction)
The Stackelberg model (firm asymmetry)	The Edgeworth model (with capacity restriction)

CDs to the sale of digital files on platforms such as Spotify. The market for physical CDs where production capacity is limited could be represented by the Edgeworth model, while the new Spotify market, whose production capacity is unlimited, would be better represented by the Bertrand model.

There are two forms of collusion: explicit agreements and tacit agreements.

Forming a cartel can increase the profits of companies because they take into account how each of their decisions affects the profits of others.

The ability to reach an agreement is "realistic" if time is taken into account (repeated interactions between firms).

Firms do not always get along because of the opportunities for cheating that trigger price wars.

The possibility of collusion is facilitated by several factors: the small number of firms, the importance of the weight placed on future profits, the existence of barriers to entry, contacts in several markets, cost asymmetries, and the lack of uncertainty in demand.

The conditions for the formation of agreements can be the following: small number of suppliers, low price elasticity of demand, little fluctuation in demand and high fixed costs, barriers to entry, homogeneity of firms in terms of production costs, and homogeneity of firms in terms of products.

4.6 Suggested Questions

1. In a duopoly, Cournot equilibrium occurs when both firms

   a. Are price takers.
   b. Collide in a cartel.
   c. Have the ability to simultaneously affect the price of the good.
   d. Differentiate products.

2. In a duopoly, the Edgeworth equilibrium occurs when both companies

   a. Compete in quantity.
   b. Have production limitations.
   c. Have symmetrical behavior.
   d. None of the above.

3. Bertrand's paradox means that:

    a. Both companies collude.
    b. They have the competitive monopoly price.
    c. Both companies have zero profits.
    d. One firm has more information than the other.

4. When analyzing a market, it is observed that the equilibrium quantity and price coincide for a long period of time with the quantity and price that correspond to the monopoly, but in the aforementioned market, several companies operate, from the supply. It can be said that it is:

    a. A bilateral monopoly.
    b. A noncooperative oligopoly.
    c. A cartel.
    d. None of the above.

5. Oligopoly differs from monopolistic competition because in oligopoly

    a. There is product differentiation.
    b. There are barriers to entry.
    c. There are no barriers to entry.
    d. The demand curves faced by the firm have a negative slope.

6. Models that are exclusively price competition include:

    a. Bertrand model and Edgeworth model.
    b. Cournot model and Cartel model.
    c. Bertrand model and Stackelberg model.
    d. There are only models of quantity competition.

7. In cartels, the group of companies seeks to:

    a. Maximize joint revenue.
    b. Maximize joint profit.
    c. Behave independently.
    d. Increase consumer surplus.

8. The Stackelberg model is more appropriate than the Cournot model in situations where:

    a. There are more than two firms.
    b. All firms enter the market simultaneously.

c. One firm makes its output decision before the other.
d. Firms are likely to collude.

9. When firms are symmetric, that is, they have the same costs, then:

    a. The Stackelberg solution is more efficient than the Cournot solution (higher total quantity, lower price).
    b. The Cournot solution is more efficient than the Stackelberg solution (higher total quantity, lower price).
    c. The Cournot and Stackelberg solutions are the same (same total quantity, same price).
    d. No solution can be found.

10. Solve: The inverse demand curve for the bicycle market is given by $P = 100 - Q$, where $Q = q1 + q2$, and the cost of each firm is given by $C(q_i) = 20q_i + \frac{q_i^2}{2}, i = 1.2$.

    a. Determine the reaction curves.
    b. Determine the Cournot equilibrium.
    c. Determine the Stackelberg equilibrium.

PART II

Market Dynamics: Contract Theory and Competition Policy

CHAPTER 5

Contract Theory

Consumers generally do not know the complete set of sellers offering the same good in a market, let alone the prices each one charge. In addition, as pointed out in Chap. 3, consumers have difficulty observing the quality of those goods. The presence of poorly informed consumers and well-informed consumers explains the price dispersion, even when dealing with identical goods. However, the Internet facilitates the search for information through comparison sites, which makes prices less dispersed. Likewise, producers are unable to observe consumers' reservation prices.

In other words, consumers and producers have incomplete information since they rarely have access to the market's data set.

In this context, information economics deals with information asymmetries in competitive markets. In addition, this field studies contracts that can be negotiated to find an equilibrium with incomplete information; that is, contract theory tries to determine optimal contracts endogenously.

Contract theory, also known as contract economics, has been developed since the 1970s as an *alternative to market theory*, based on the Walrasian model. This theory, as a framework for contractual coordination, proposes two alternative modes of coordination distinct from market coordination. In this sense, the starting point is the limitations of the general equilibrium

C. Lanchimba, *Industrial Organization*,
https://doi.org/10.1007/978-3-032-10906-4_5

theory,[1] where there is a centralization of individual behavior, that is, the interaction is achieved at a global level. Unlike this, the models of the contract theory are about partial equilibrium models[2] and formal or informal but explicit contracts (Shapiro and Varian 2000). Therefore, these are bilateral agreements with decentralized interaction.

For an economist, a contract is an agreement in which two parties mutually define and commit to specific behaviors. Therefore, a contract serves as a bilateral coordination mechanism, whereas the market functions as a multilateral coordination system. A contract is a binding agreement between two parties that clearly defines their respective obligations. It specifically outlines the payment mechanism that the economic agent will receive for their efforts. Therefore, it can only be based on verifiable variables, that is, those that can be evaluated by an external and independent agent, which guarantees compliance with the contract.

Using verifiable variables in a contract allows each party to present its case in court with evidence if a breach of contract occurs. If there is no information asymmetry between the agents who sign a contract, then the problem admits a trivial solution. In other words, it is about writing a complete contract that moderates the behavior of all agents in each of the possible scenarios. No party can deviate from the contract, as the regulator or legal system can fully detect any breach and impose sanctions if necessary.

The problem becomes nontrivial when there is information asymmetry since it is not possible to establish a verifiable agreement. In this case, it is virtually impossible to implement an optimal allocation of property rights and royalties. The solution is, then, a so-called "second best" contract, which establishes the best organizational mechanism to mitigate excessive earnings arising from one party's informational advantage.

The economics of contracts includes three competing and complementary contract theories: (i) the incentive theory (agency theory), (ii) the theory of transaction costs, and (iii) the theory of incomplete contracts.

[1] Walrasian model in perfect competition, where it is assumed that in the market of values, goods, and production factors, equilibrium prices and quantities are determined simultaneously.

[2] Determination of equilibrium prices and quantities in a market independent of other markets.

5.1 AGENCY THEORY

Agency theory or incentive theory emphasizes the principal-agent paradigm. The works of Laffont and Martimort (2001), Bernard Salanié (2005), and Bolton and Dewatripont (2005) have undoubtedly provided guidelines for the development of this theory.

The principal-agent paradigm deals with the bilateral or agency relationship where one of the parties contractually delegates (principal) to another (agent) an action or decision. It is thus understood as a form of delegation that substitutes a market transaction with a contractual arrangement. The principal takes the initiative to propose a contract, defining its terms. If the agent accepts it, the utility derived from this contract is higher than the reservation utility, which is the utility they would achieve by not signing the contract. This relationship can be understood as a shareholder-manager, employer-employee, or franchisor-franchisee relationship, where the manager, employee, or franchisee performs actions that directly influence the principal's profits.

In the initial model, the agent does not oppose the principal (no bilateral negotiation). If the agent does not sign the contract, the relationship does not take place. On the contrary, if the agent accepts, he considers the terms of the agreement and commits to act under the contract. This relationship can be understood as a shareholder-manager, employer-employee, or franchisor-franchisee relationship, where the manager, employee, or franchisee performs actions that directly influence the principal's profits.

According to Laffont (2006), agency theory is a simplification of game theory.[3] Since agency problems eliminate the bargaining problem, the principal has the power to build the rules of the game. We consider this situation as a Stackelberg equilibria in which the principal is the leader.

If there is no asymmetric information between the group members and if there is more than one external control agent (such as a court), the answer is to write a complete and contingent contract that will guide everyone's behavior in all possible states of nature, i.e., no one can break it under penalty of being sanctioned by the court.

[3] In game theory, the equilibrium that players adopt in a strategic environment is predetermined. In contrast, contract theory argues for the existence of a strategic environment designed to incentivize players to behave in a specific way. The question, then, is how the strategic environment can be modified—whether through a contract or an organizational structure—to ensure that the players' equilibrium is effective.

In this context, the problem becomes interesting if there is information asymmetry or contracts cannot contemplate all possible situations. In the case of information asymmetry, there is no solution in terms of an optimal contract (equilibrium). However, equilibrium in this case would be the second best solution. In general, the agent has more information than the principal. Thus, this theory studies the behavior of agents when faced with information acquisition. Information asymmetry reveals two key problems: anti-selection or adverse selection, which relates to hidden information (*Adverse selection*), and moral hazard, which concerns the study of hidden actions (*Moral hazard*).

5.1.1 Basic Model

The basic model considers symmetric information, which describes a relationship between two people, companies, or institutions. The outcome is random and depends in part on the effort of the economic agent A. Both participants have the same information when the relationship is established and afterward.

Natural conditions determine the state of the world, i.e., it is an exogenous behavioral characteristic of A. This situation is a contractual relationship with symmetric information. In other words, nature intervenes after the activity of the principal P but also after that of A.

A and P are in the same position relative to the randomness of nature. In this model, A's remuneration is defined by an optimal distribution of risk between P and A. Both the agent and the principal can be *risk neutral*, meaning they are indifferent between a fixed income and an uncertain income with the same expected utility, willingly accepting income variability. They could also be *risk averse,* in which case the agent prefers a given income to a risky income with the same utility (in this particular case, it has a diminishing marginal utility), and the individual will look for insurance. Finally, they could be *risk lovers,* individuals who have a preference for taking risks. They prefer an uncertain income over a given level of income, even if the expected value of that uncertain income is lower than that of a certain level of income.

On the one hand, if P is risk neutral and A is risk averse, the contract should stipulate that A receives a fixed salary for participating in the relationship; this salary is independent of the results but depends on the characteristics of the work performed and the effort supplied (so the risk is assumed by P). On the other hand, if A is risk neutral and P is risk averse, the optimal contract is a franchise contract in which A pays a fixed amount to P and receives in return the result of the relationship (A suffers risk but becomes a residual claimant). If A and P are risk averse, the contract defines an optimal distribution of risk between A and P based on their degree of risk aversion.

5.1.1.1 *The Principal Maximization Problem*

For P, the Pareto optimal remuneration scheme is of the form

$$max \, \Sigma_{i=1}^{n} \pi(e) B(x_i - w(x_i))$$

subject to $\Sigma_{i=1}^{n} \pi(e) u(w(x_i)) \geq \underline{U}$, with $\pi(e) = P(x = x_i/e)$
where x is the set of possible outcomes and e is the effort expended by A. $\pi(e) = P(x = x_i/e) \; i = 1, .., n$ is the state of nature. Also, $B(x_i - w(x_i))$ is the utility function of P, $B' > 0$ and $B'' \leq 0$; $U(w, e) = u(w) - v(e)$ is the utility function of A, $u' > 0$; $u'' \geq 0$ and $v' > 0$; $v'' \geq 0$ (disutility of effort[4]); and $\underline{U}$ is the reservation utility.

The constraint $\Sigma_{i=1}^{n} \pi(e) u(w(x_i)) \geq \underline{U}$ states that A does not participate in the contract if his gain is less than the disutility of effort or his reservation utility. This contract is based on two elements: e, observable or verifiable, and the wage w that w depends on the outcome. The optimization is done through the Kuhn-Tucker theorem, since the constraint is an inequality, λ is added instead of subtracted as in a usual maximization model:

$$L(w(x_i), e, \lambda) = \Sigma_{i=1}^{n} \pi(e) B(x_i - w(x_i)) +$$
$$\lambda[\Sigma_{i=1}^{n} \pi(e) u(w(x_i)) - v(e) - u]$$

We maximize this amount in the derivative of the function $w(x_i)$ and set it equal to 0 (the function is of the form $f(g(x))$, derivative $f'(g(x)\Delta g'(x))$, where

$$\frac{dL}{dw = 0} \Leftrightarrow -\pi(e) B'(x_i - w(x_i)) + \lambda \pi(e) u'(w(x_i)) = 0$$

[4] Personal cost of effort. It is an increasing function that tends to infinity.

$$\lambda = \frac{B'(x_i - w(x_i))}{u'(w(x_i))}.$$

In this case, $\pi(e)$ disappears in the simplification, $B'(x_i - w(x_i))$ is the marginal utility of $P(> 0)$, and $u'(w(x_i))$ is the marginal utility of $A(> 0)$.

We can conclude that $\lambda > 0$ is the measure of the sensitivity of P's utility to a variation in the reservation utility and that the participation constraint A gets saturated in equilibrium. Consequently, the optimal contract is to define $w(x_i)$, given the position of A and P concerning risk. The optimal contract is a contract that offers the following conditions:

$$\frac{B'(x_i - w(x_i))}{u'(w(x_i))} = constant$$

This condition will not have the same form as the position regarding the risk of A and P. Furthermore, the proportion of marginal utilities must be constant, i.e., we have a constant marginal rate of substitution, which is the classical Pareto condition. In other words, the marginal rate of substitution is represented by the tangent line to the indifference curve, which remains constant at equilibrium and matches the price ratio of the consumer's budget line.

Accordingly, in the symmetric model, P signs a contract with A that stipulates that the latter must exert a certain level of effort or make certain decisions in exchange for remuneration. The level of effort is fixed by P, is verifiable by him, and is constant during the contract. P and A have the same information (in their respective utility function and behavior, among others). Furthermore, only the "behavior" of nature is uncertain.

In this context, the problems of the principal-agent relationship under information asymmetry are outlined below.

5.1.2 *Adverse Selection*

When individuals are uncertain about the content or quality of the product, certain companies may abuse this situation by passing off poor-quality items as good. This situation produces a market failure since it is an opportunistic behavior. Consumers cannot distinguish a poor-quality product from a good one since companies producing poor-quality products do everything to hide information, forcing many high-quality producers to

Table 5.1 Problem to solve. Source: Author

Good-quality products	Poor-quality products
Half of the vehicles	The other half
$Q = 20{,}000$ $U_a = 20{,}000 - P$ $U_v = P - 20{,}000$	$Q = 10{,}000$

withdraw from the market. Specifically, the impact of information problems on market functioning arises from one participant's inability to observe a key characteristic of the good, leading to incomplete and asymmetric information.

In other words, buyers' ability to assess the quality of the goods they intend to purchase is limited. Sellers have an incentive to exaggerate the quality of their products to maximize their selling price. Buyers, therefore, cannot trust sellers' statements nor deduce that a higher price means good quality. In this sense, price is no longer a perfect signal of the value of the good since consumers can obtain different quality goods for the same price.

Ackerlof (1970) explains that in the second-hand vehicle market, the suppliers know the quality of the goods. However, this quality is not observable to the buyers. Instead, buyers are aware of the distribution of product quality. In the case of only two quality levels (good and bad), each buyer knows the proportion of good and bad vehicles in the market. The sellers cannot signal the quality of their goods since there is a unique price p. Likewise, the buyers are identical and obtain the utility $U_a = Q - P$ (difference between quality and price) from their purchase, while the sellers' utility is $U_v = P - Q$. In this context, the following scenario is as follows. See Table 5.1.

This situation can be resolved in the context of symmetric and asymmetric information. In the case of a symmetric information situation, cars are exchanged at their fair value, i.e., good cars are exchanged at \$20,000 and bad cars at \$10,000. In this case, it would be a first-rank optimal equilibrium.

On the other hand, in a situation of asymmetric information, buyers refuse to buy a car at \$20,000, knowing that half of them are of poor quality and can be of poor quality with a probability of 0.5, where the expected utility derived from the purchase price of P is as follows: $[(0.5 \times 20{,}000) + (0.5 \times 10{,}000)] - P = 15{,}000 - P$.

But for \$15,000, buyers know that sellers of good-quality cars are making losses of (−5,000) and refuse to sell. So, for \$15,000, only low-quality cars are sold. Given this situation, buyers refuse to pay more than \$10,000 for these cars. Therefore, only low-quality vehicles are traded at that price, and good-quality cars are left out of the market, "adverse selection." Consequently, an adverse selection situation eliminates trades of good-quality products. In an extreme case, anti-selection eliminates all trade.

So, anti-selection events come from an asymmetry in the type of agents, i.e., intrinsic quality. This scenario is counterproductive for "good" agents.

The game then becomes about finding a mechanism to prompt the informed party to reveal private information that it possesses, i.e., to encourage the informed party to disclose its type, known as the ***disclosure principle***. The disclosure principle assumes that the agent has revealed its type, not directly, but through its choice from a menu of contracts (e.g., choosing between a high- or low-deductible premium car insurance contract). The menu of contracts should be such that an agent has a higher utility by revealing its type than by hiding the principal.

The menu of contracts is the solution to this type of problem and is referred to as a "separation contract," designed to incentivize the agent to reveal their true type. Separation contracts are based on the disclosure principle. For example, the seller may introduce a long-term warranty on the second-hand vehicle for sale. Poor sellers are reluctant to incorporate such a clause, refuse the warranty, and thus reveal their type.

5.1.2.1 *The Principal Maximization Problem*

The utility function depends on the participants' risk aversion in the game. The *von Neumann-Morgenstern* (VNM) utility function is the utility function under conditions of uncertainty. It is a formulation adopted from the utility in choice modeling when events are probabilistic.

The degree of concavity of the VNM utility function illustrates the degree of risk aversion of the agent. When the definition of expected utility is applied, the utility function of the participants is of the expected VNM type, and the utility is the sum of the utilities associated with all possible events, weighted by the probability of occurrence.

In this context, the utility function of A is

$$U(w, e) = u(w) - v(e)$$

where w is the remuneration of A and e is its level of effort ($u' > 0 \quad u'' \leq 0$ and $v' > 0 \quad v'' \geq 0$[5]). Furthermore, $\pi(e)$ is the probability of having x_i with effort e. Finally, the result of the agency relationship is as follows: $\pi(e). = .simbol\ of\ summation\ from\ 1\ to\ n\ Pi(e)Xi$ is an increasing ($\pi' \geq 0$) and concave ($\pi'' \leq 0$) function.

In this context, we assume that there are two types of agents: (i) a type that has an effort disutility $v(e)$, G (the good type), and (ii) a type that has an effort disutility, $kv(e)$ ($k \epsilon R$ and greater than 1), B (the bad type).

The disutility of agent B's effort is

$$U^G(w, e) = u(w) - v(e). \tag{5.1.1}$$

Equation (5.1.1) is higher than that of agent G:

$$U^B(w, e) = u(w) - kv(e) \tag{5.1.2}$$

In other words, for the same level of effort, the principal will have to pay more to B (cost of higher effort) (See Eq. 5.1.2).

The optimal contract is the one that maximizes the expected benefit of the principal, given the constraints. The objective of the contract menu is to induce G to make a greater effort than e^B (the level chosen if there is no discriminating contract) while making contract B less attractive to G (decreasing w with e).

$$Max_q(\pi(e^G) - w^G) + (1 - q)(\pi(e^B) - w^B)$$

subject to

$$u(w^G) - v(e^G) \geq \underline{U}$$

$$u(w^B) - kv(e^B) \geq \underline{U}$$

$$u(w^G) - v(e^G) \geq u(w^B) - v(e^B)$$

$$u(w^B) - kv(e^B) \geq u(w^G) - kv(e^G)$$

where q is the probability estimated by P that the agent is of type G. $\underline{U}$ is the reservation utility, and $\pi(e)$ is the result of the agency relationship.

[5] Disutility of effort.

The constraints of the maximization problem are divided into two:

(i) Participation constraints, since there are two types of agents and two possible contracts:

$$u(w^G) - v(e^G) \geq \underline{U}$$

$$u(w^B) - kv(e^B) \geq \underline{U}$$

(ii) Disclosure restrictions (or self-selection):

$$u(w^G) - v(e^G) \geq u(w^B) - v(e^B)$$

$$u(w^B) - kv(e^B) \geq u(w^G) - kv(e^G)$$

These restrictions make the contract discriminatory, which is interesting because it is a mechanism for revealing the type of agency. However, the latter has a cost borne by the *good* agents who obtain a level of utility lower than that of the first-rank optimum.

5.1.3 *Adverse Selection: Signaling Theory*

Knowing that there are two producers in the market offering products of different qualities, the companies that sell high-quality products must adopt a signaling strategy. The signal sent before the exchange by the *good* agents is to inform their type. The signal is credible in the eyes of consumers only if the cost is lower for the good agents than for the *bad* ones, which implies this signal must not be imitable by companies that produce low-quality products. Like separating contracts, the signal is costly, for example, the signal of having a diploma in the labor market. So, the *good* agents are still at a disadvantage due to information asymmetries.

Spence (1973) describes a wage relationship, where an employee can signal that he works hard and is intelligent. One possible message is that he earned a diploma unrelated to his profession, reflecting his open-mindedness. Additionally, his achievement demonstrates hard work, as he graduated while training in a different field.

Another example of this situation can be an experience good whose quality can be known only after the purchase and after its use or consumption. If the product is of good quality, buyers will continue repurchasing it; otherwise, they will stop if the quality is poor. In this case, a credible information strategy can be to sell at a loss a product launch to maximize customer trials or offer a money-back guarantee to reassure buyers in case of dissatisfaction. Only a company with good-quality products can carry out this type of promotion since it knows it can recover its momentary losses later. Similarly, an intensive advertising campaign or the offer of a guarantee is a way of indicating the quality of the product. Not only advertising represents a way of artificially differentiating the product, but it is also a means of reducing information asymmetries between consumers and companies.

5.1.4 *Moral Hazard*

In the market, many companies can imperfectly observe the characteristics and behavior of consumers. As a result, consumers may behave abusively or opportunistically. In other words, companies can face a moral hazard problem. For example, a buyer whose product has a warranty may be less careful because he will receive compensation in case of damage. These problems are mainly evident in the insurance market, where the insured may have the temptation to engage in riskier behavior. To avoid and reduce this problem, companies can offer customers incentive contracts that lead them to maintain appropriate behavior, for example, in the case of guarantees, companies can impose suspension clauses in case of inappropriate service use.

Specifically, moral hazard emerges when there are hidden actions that the principal cannot observe. Therefore, there is an asymmetry of information, and the problem is then to encourage the agent with private information to make an optimal decision for the principal. The agent's action affects the principal, but the latter does not observe the action. The principal observes the outcome but cannot determine whether it is a result of the agent's actions or external factors. In other words, he observes the result and the action but cannot evaluate the relationship between the two variables.

In contrast to the basic model of agency theory, in the moral hazard model, *A* makes a decision ("action") that affects his utility and that of *P*. *P* observes only the "outcome," which is an imperfect signal of the action taken. The action spontaneously chosen by *A* is not Pareto-Optimal. Uncertainty in the contractual relationship is not entirely asymmetric; it stems from two sources. One is symmetric, related to the state of nature, while the other is asymmetric derived from *A*'s behavior. From *P*'s point

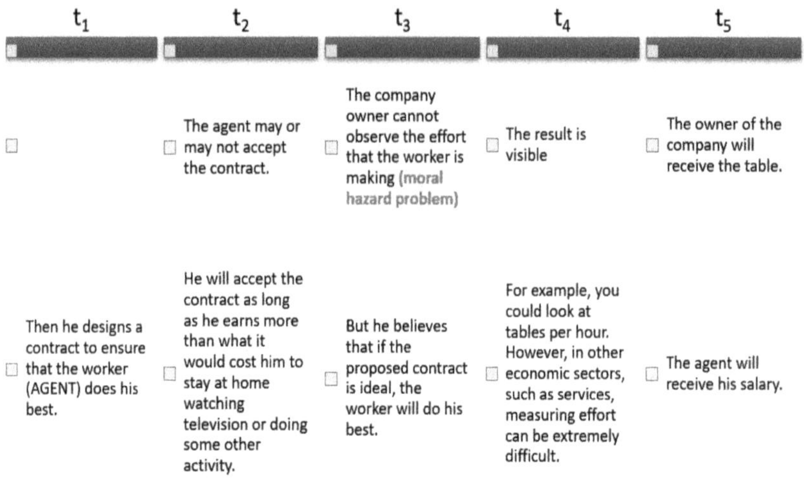

Fig. 5.1 Moral hazard problem. Source: Author

of view, the two uncertainties are inseparable, since P cannot know which uncertainty explains the outcome x observed by P. Consequently, a clause regarding A's behavior without knowing which behavior generates the outcome should not be included in the contract.

In an employment contract illustrated in Fig. 5.1, it is common that the level of effort exerted by the employee (or party) is not verifiable. Therefore, this contract should not include a clause such as " If I determine that you have put in significant effort, your pay will be higher than if your effort is minimum." It is almost impossible for a firm to prove that the employee's level of effort was below their full potential.

In a moral hazard situation, if A has a fixed remuneration, he engages in opportunistic behavior because his remuneration is independent of the level of effort. P can anticipate this risk and offer a fixed pay contract, where he chooses the pay level that exactly compensates A for his minimum effort level.

Let w be A's remuneration, $\underline{u}$ be A's reservation utility, $v(e_{min})$ be the disutility level of minimum effort, and $w_{min} = u^{-1}(\underline{u} + v(e_{min}))$, the minimum remuneration. In this case, w_{min} is inefficient since it does not allow associating w with the observed level of effort. The problem remains the same if we set a variable w_{min} based on the results. However, we cannot be certain whether this result is driven by the level of effort of *e* or simply by a favorable environment The situation will not have the *first-best* situation if *P* can observe all of *A*'s actions. In this case, we can force *A* to choose the most efficient action and then choose the salaries that make an optimal distribution of risks between the two parties.

It is often assumed in this case that *P* is risk neutral (we can justify this hypothesis by the fact that *P* can diversify the risks related to his relationship with *A*). However, *A* is risk averse (being "small" makes it more difficult to diversify the risk). The optimal distribution of risk assumes that *P* "fully insures" *A* by paying a constant salary and bearing all the risks related to their common activity.

If *P* is risk neutral, the first-best optimum involves providing *A* with a fixed salary. However, this situation encourages *A* to choose the less expensive action for him, which is not optimal in general, and leads to a second-rank situation. The solution to the moral hazard problem assumes that *P* offers *A* a contract that balances insurance where *A*'s wage is only partially dependent on the outcome and incentives, which motivate *P* to tie wages to performance. On the other hand, if *A* is risk neutral, there is no arbitrage. We can assume that all risks align and that the second-best outcome coincides with the first best (*P* selling to firm *A*); however, this scenario has limited practical relevance.

5.1.4.1 Moral Hazard Problem

The goal is to determine the level of effort exerted by *A*, which directly influences their compensation. Meanwhile, *P* consistently aims to maximize their expected profit:

$$Max \sum_{i=1}^{n} \pi(e) B(x_i - w(x_i))$$

Furthermore, *A*'s participation constraint takes the following form,

$$(i) \sum_{i=1}^{n} \pi(e) u(w(x_i) - v(e)) \geq \underline{u}$$

and the incentive constraint of *A*, who seeks to maximize the utility of his expected income, that is, the effort level *e* such that

$$(ii)\, e = ArgMax \sum_{i=1}^{n} \pi(e)u(w(x_i) - v(e)).$$

This expression is A's incitement constraint, which is the value of the variable e for which the function U reaches its maximum, where x_i is the possible outcome among n.

So, we have an optimization problem with two constraints (i) and (ii): the incitement constraint (ii) is itself an optimization program ($MaxU$ under the constraint that e reaches a certain value). The idea is then to transform the incitement constraint to solve it, but there is no unique solution.

Suppose that $e \epsilon E$ is the set of possible effort levels, and we look for an e in E that maximizes the incitement constraint. Thus, the maximization problem depends on the form E; it has three possible strategies:

- $E = \underline{e}, e'$, classify the effort in two levels (Harris and Raviv 1979).
- $E = \underline{e}, e'$, there is an infinite solution between these two levels of effort, $\pi(e) = e\pi^H + (1-e)\pi^L$, with $\pi \epsilon [0, 1]$, but that assumes a continuity condition on the marginal properties of the effort. The linear constraint is unlikely. So, it is an approximation of the continuous level of effort with linear constraint (Hart and Holmstrom 1987).
- Replacing $Maxf(x)$ in the incentive constraint by a first-order condition, namely that the first derivative of the incentive function is a first-order approach (Holmstrom 1979).

We will now see that the first approximation is possible.

Agent Chooses Between Two Effort Levels Suppose that P is risk neutral and that A is risk averse to temporarily putting aside the risk-sharing problem. We can then characterize the impact of asymmetric information by comparing the structure of the optimal contract under asymmetry to that of the optimal contract with full information. Any deviation from the reference contract will explain the existence of moral hazard. In this context, A chooses between two effort levels, e^H (high effort) and e^L (low effort).

Suppose for simplicity that $x_1 < x_2 < \ldots < x_n$ (we arrange the results from lowest (Eq. 5.1.4) to highest (Eq. 5.1.3)), and look for the highest index i. Thus,

$$\pi^H = p\left(x = \frac{x_i}{e} = e^H\right) \tag{5.1.3}$$

and

$$\pi^L = p\left(x = \frac{x_i}{e} = e^L\right). \tag{5.1.4}$$

For every effort, $\pi^H \cong 0$ and $\pi^L \cong 0$; $\bigvee i = 1, \ldots, n$, there exists a nondisclosure condition, where P cannot deduce the level of e knowing x_i.

According to the definition of first-order stochastic dominance, a random variable x is said to dominate another random variable y if it is preferred by all individuals whose utility function increases with wealth.

Then the following first-order stochastic dominance condition is

$$\sum_{i=1}^{k} \pi^H < \sum_{i=1}^{k} \pi^L$$

$k = 1, \ldots, n - 1.$

Explanation

$p(x \leq \frac{k}{e^H}) < p(x \leq \frac{k}{e^L})$
$\Leftrightarrow 1 - p(x > \frac{k}{e^H}) < 1 - p(x > \frac{k}{e^L})$
$\Leftrightarrow p(x > \frac{k}{e^H}) > (x > \frac{k}{e^L})$

This inequality reflects the idea that bad outcomes are more likely when A is lazy than when he is not, i.e., it is more likely that outcomes are higher than x_i (for all $k < n$) when the effort is high than when the effort is low.

Suppose that $v(e^H) > v(e^L)$, then the disutility of e is stronger when e is high. P looks for the highest index i of x.

The following observations pertain to the level of effort required by P:

- If P demands e^L, the moral hazard problem does not arise. This occurs, for instance, when the randomness of nature is so high that P chooses a fixed remuneration contract assuming that A will produce e^L.
- In general, we offer A a fixed remuneration; P is sure that A will produce the minimum level of effort. This effort maximizes A's utility (minimizes the disutility of effort).

- In that case, P pays A $w^L = u^{-1}(\underline{u} + v(e^L))$ (case 1 of the symmetric information model). This contract under symmetric information is optimal here.
- The most interesting case occurs if P asks A for e^H (true when x_i increases passing e^H). In this case, if P continues to propose a fixed payoff, A will choose an effort e^L. Then, to obtain e^H, P finds a contract where the payoff A depends on the outcome. The incentive constraint is as follows:

$$\Sigma_{i=1}^{n}\pi^{H}u(w(x_i) - v(e^H)) \geq \Sigma_{i=1}^{n}\pi^{L}u(w(x_i) - v(e^L))$$

Last equation means that the incentive constraint is stronger if e^H, where there is dependence of w on x_i.

$\Sigma_{i=1}^{n}\pi^{H}u(w(x_i))$ is determined when the expected utility of VNM, $v(e^H)$, is true. To expect A to make an effort e^H, the constraint must be $\geq$. Thus, we can rewrite the constraint as this:

$$\Sigma_{i=1}^{n}(\pi^{H} - \pi^{L})u(w(x_i)) \geq v(e^H) - v(e^L)$$

where $(\pi^H - \pi^L)$ is the measure of increase in effort, $\Sigma_{i=1}^{n}(\pi^{H} - \pi^{L})u(w(x_i))$ is the gain in utility linked to effort-related growth, and $v(e^H) - v(e^L)$ is the growth in disutility from effort.

The optimal calculation for A to choose a high level of effort is

$$Max\sum_{i=1}^{n}\pi^{H}(x_i - w(x_i))$$

subject to participation restriction:

$$(i)\sum_{i=1}^{n}\pi^{H}u(w(x_i)) - v(e^H) \geq \underline{u}$$

and the restriction incitement:

$$(ii)\sum_{i=1}^{n}(\pi^{H} - \pi^{L})u(w(x_i)) \geq v(e^H) - v(e^L).$$

It is observed that:

- The function $B()$ is unnecessary because P is risk neutral. Since B is assumed to be linear, its specific form does not affect P's utility. Instead, P's utility depends solely on the outcomes related to agent H.
- The participation constraint is applied only to the effort level e^H, since agent must participate.
- Finally, the effort is no longer optimized thanks to the incentive constraint (which is no longer $Argmax$).
- The optimization program seeks $w(x_i)$ once the utility function P is maximized under the participation constraint and the incentive of A.

The maximization problem is written as this:

$$L(w(x_i), e, \lambda, \mu) = \sum_{i=1}^{n} \pi^H (x_i - w(x_i))$$

$$+\lambda \left[\sum_{i=1}^{n} \pi^H u(w(x_i)) - v(e^H) - \underline{u} \right]$$

$$+\mu \left[\Sigma_{i=1}^{n} (\pi^H - \pi^L) u(w(x_i)) - v(e^H) + v(e^L) \right]$$

where $\pi^H (x_i - w(x_i))$ is the maximization of the function P that depends only on H. We introduce an intermediate step on the symmetric model, which is to reflect on the value of μ, $\mu \neq 0$.

μ is the measure of the sensitivity of income to the variation of the level of effort from e^H to e^L. In other words, μ is a measure of moral hazard. If $\mu = 0$, there is no moral hazard problem; it is a symmetric model. Then, the Lagrangian is derived as a function of the wage $w(x_i)$ for all $i = 1, .., n$:

$$\frac{\delta L}{\delta w(x_i)} = 0$$

$$\Leftrightarrow -\pi^H + \lambda \pi^H u'(w(x_i)) + \mu (p_i^H - \pi^L) u'(w(x_i)) = 0.$$

$w'(x_i)$ vanishes because the three functions are divided by $w'(x_i)$, so we have:

$$\frac{\pi^H}{u'(w(x_i))} = \lambda \pi^H + \mu (\pi^H - \pi^L) = 0.$$

By placing summations on the members of the preceding equation:

$$\sum \frac{\pi^H}{u'(w(x_i))} = \lambda \sum \pi^H + \sum \mu(\pi^H - p_i^L) = 0$$

with $\sum \pi^H = 1$ y $(\pi^H - \pi^L) = 0$, we have:

$$\sum \frac{\pi^H}{u'(w(x_i))} = \lambda.$$

The question is whether $\lambda > 0$ to have a saturated condition. By hypothesis, it is known that $\pi^H > 0$ and $u'(w(x_i)) > 0$ (otherwise, the marginal utility of w is constant). Then, we can conclude that $\lambda > 0$, and the participation restriction is saturated in equilibrium (this result is obtained by assuming that utility is additive and separable).

Rewriting the derivative of the Lagrangian:

$$\sum \frac{\pi^H}{u'(w(x_i))} = \lambda\pi^H + \mu(\pi^H - \pi^L).$$

Thus, an optimal contract equation is obtained:

$$\sum \frac{1}{u'(w(x_i))} = \lambda\pi^H + \mu\left(1 - \frac{\pi^L}{\pi^H}\right)$$

In this case, we want to know if $\mu > 0$. In fact, if $\mu = 0$, we have constant $u'(w(x_i))$. This framework would be a symmetric information model, so there is no moral hazard problem. The Kuhn-Tucker theorem dictates that μ is nonnegative, so it is $\mu > 0$.

$\mu > 0$ means that the existence of the moral hazard problem implies a strictly positive cost for P. Furthermore, the gain P is strictly greater when the information about the effort is symmetric (μ disappears) than in a moral hazard situation.

The wage gap between symmetric information and moral hazard reflects the information asymmetry held by A. For A, when $\mu > 0$, the wage varies depending on the outcome. $\frac{\pi^L}{\pi^H}$ is the likelihood ratio, which indicates how well the outcome serves as a signal of the high effort level e^H. It is weaker than π^H but strong relative to π^L.

In this case, the probability that A produces e^H is high. A reduction in the likelihood ratio implies an increase in the probability that $e = e^H$ when the observed wage is $w(x_i)$.

In summary, P pays A based on the outcome for three reasons:

i Only the outcome is observable, and P proposes to base his contract on verifiable variables that affect A's behavior.
ii To give A an incentive.
iii P seeks a balance between the incentives given to A, but they are costly for P and the risk hedge, which tends to make w fixed (incentive and hedge are contradictory, because one cannot simultaneously encourage and hedge completely).

Recapitulating the optimal contract equation as follows:

$$\frac{1}{u'(w(x_i))} = \lambda + \mu(1 - \frac{\pi^L}{\pi^H}) \quad i = ..n$$

$\Leftrightarrow$

$$u'(w(x_i)) = \frac{1}{\lambda + \mu(1 - \frac{\pi^L}{\pi^H})}$$

$\Leftrightarrow$

$$w(x_i) = (u')^{-1} \frac{1}{\lambda + \mu(1 - \frac{\pi^L}{\pi^H})}$$

This expression is the optimal wage equation, in which it is possible to distinguish three cases:

i For the results, x_i such that $\pi^H = \pi^L$, we have $w(x_i) = (u')^{-1}(\frac{1}{\lambda}) = \overline{w}$ constant, which is the reference value.
ii For outcomes x_i such that $\frac{\pi^L}{\pi^H} > 1$, we have $w(x_i) < \overline{w}$ (u' is decreasing).
iii For outcomes x_i such that $\frac{\pi^L}{\pi^H} < 1$ (in other words, it is more likely that $e = e^H$), we have $w(x_i) > \overline{w}$.

5.2 Vertical Restraints

5.2.1 *Introduction*

Vertical restraints are contractual clauses that link firms at different levels of the distribution chain, such as distributors or wholesalers and retailers. These contractual arrangements differ from linear pricing, where the distributor pays the supplier a monetary amount proportional to the quantities purchased in standard microeconomic theory.

The main forms of vertical restraints are presented in Table 5.2.

On the other hand, Rey and Caballero-Sanz (1996) classify vertical restrictions into three categories:

- Restrictions affecting the payment regime, including nonlinear pricing, fees, and commissions.
- Restrictions limiting the distributor's rights, such as floor and ceiling prices, imposed resale quantities, exclusive distribution, and tied sales.
- Restrictions limiting the rights of both parties, such as territorial exclusivity

The focus of researchers on this type of contract is justified by two key factors: (i) Its importance in the current configuration of industrial relations, where networks occupy an important place in the distribution activity. The modes of distribution have undergone profound changes; in that sense, the organization in networks is an important innovation in industrial organization. (ii) Because they are the subject of a recurring debate in competition policy (Comanor and Rey 1997 and Kay 1990), incentive theory and the principal-agent paradigm have offered a unique perspective—one that now underpins the competition laws of both the United States and the European Union.

Thus, incentive theory and the principal-agent paradigm are generally considered to be clear theoretical framework for the analysis of vertical constraints.

In this context, a series of studies focused on private and social interests, vertical constraints, their motives, and their welfare consequences have been developed since the mid-1980s (Mathewson and Winter 1984, 1985; P. Rey and J. Tirole 1986; J. Tirole 1988).

In general, the framework used is a producer distributing its products through an intermediary distributor or distributors. The pair formed by the upstream and downstream firms is a vertical structure (See Table 5.2).

Table 5.2 General typology of vertical restraints. Source: Author

Instrument	Vertical constraint
Price Wholesale prices (p_w) for 1 and 2 or consumer price (p) by 3	*Nonlinear tariff:* The amount paid by the distributor (T) is not proportional to the quantity purchased from the supplier (q) : $T(q) \neq p_w q$, as Franchise fee: fixed premium (A) and binomial tariff: $T(q) = A + p_w q$ *Rates and commissions :* are not based on the quantity purchased to the produ cer but in the total sales or benefits of the distributor *Consumer price without taxes or recommended:* (a) Ceiling price: $p \leq \overline{p}$ (b) Floor price: $p \geq \underline{p}$ (c) Fixed price: $p = \overline{p} = \underline{p}$
Quantity Intermediate quantity wholesale (q)	*Fixed quantity:* $q = \overline{q} = \underline{q}$ *Minimum quantity:* $q \geq \underline{q}$ *Rationing:* $q \leq \overline{q}$
Territory Territory of intervention of the distributor	*Territorial exclusivity* *In the spatial sense:* of a geographic region *In the sense of a customer segmentation:* by type of elasticity
Supply Product line of the distributor	*Tied sales = sale in batches*: the producer forces the distributor to sell several products of the brand, for example, the entire range of these products *Exclusive supply:* The distributor is prohibited from selling products of the competition
Characteristics of the distributor Qualitative characteristics	*Selective distribution:* the producer sells to a single buyer (exclusive distribution) or to a limited number of buyers

The producer-distributor relationship is an agency relationship in the sense that the upstream firm (the principal) delegates to the downstream firms the distribution task (agent/agents); this task directly affects the principal's profit.

Agency models constitute a microeconomic representation of contracts. The principal has the initiative of the contract and all the bargaining power (i.e., he determines the characteristics of the contract). Agency theory shows that in the absence of constraints, coordination problems (externalities) affect the efficiency of the vertical structure. Secondly, it identifies contractual clauses that eliminate these external effects. Furthermore, according to Mathewson and Winter (1984), restrictions are considered "sufficient" when they allow the decentralized vertical structure to achieve the maximum level of joint benefits.

First, we focus on the relationship between a producer and an exclusive distributor (agency model in the case of a single distributor) that allows us to analyze the problem of basic vertical externalities. Two major coordination problems are evident: (i) a problem related to the choice of the retail sale price (double marginalization, Sect. 5.2.1.1) and (ii) a problem related to the level of effort in distributors' sales (moral hazard, Sect. 5.2.2).

Next, we consider the case of a network of distributors where there is intra-brand competition among the distributors. Two externalities are considered: a basic vertical externality, to which a horizontal externality is added, introducing a *free-riding* problem (Sect. 5.2.3). We begin our analysis in a deterministic setting before considering the consequences of introducing the assumptions of uncertainty and risk aversion (Sect. 5.2.4).

5.2.1.1 *Double Marginalization*

The double marginalization problem was first addressed by Spengler (1950). At its core lies a provocative question: What is worse than a monopoly? The answer is two monopolies operating within the same distribution chain. This scenario arises when each firm in a vertical structure exercises market power, leading to inefficiencies greater than those caused by a single monopoly.

The double marginalization problem occurs when two firms independently set the prices of complementary goods. This framework can be used both in the case of traditional complements (e.g., coffee and sugar) and in the case of a vertical relationship (e.g., when the complementary goods are a manufactured product and the retail service through which the good is sold).

Note that this effect does not require perfect monopoly. Both firms must have some market power. Particularly, they must be able to price above marginal cost and achieve positive profits. If one of the two firms lacks market power, it would not make a profit, and the other firm's price setting would not have any negative externalities on that firm (at least in the long run). Therefore, double marginalization requires a certain market power on the part of both firms, but not necessarily a monopoly.

The theoretical framework here is a principal-agent problem in information symmetry. That is, both participants in the relationship are equally informed. The environment where they develop is deterministic (although there is an extension of this model with an environment involving uncertainty).

The vertical externality is basic because in this situation the benefits of the producer (*pro, Eq. 5.2.1*) and distributor (*dis, Eq. 5.2.2*) depend only on the retail sale price.

The demand function has the form $D(p) = 1 - p$, and the profit functions are the following:

$$\Pi_{pro} = pq - cq = (p_w - c)(1 - p) \tag{5.2.1}$$

$$\Pi_{dis} = (p - p_w)(1 - p) \tag{5.2.2}$$

where p_w is the producer price, p is the retail price, and c is the constant unit production cost.

When comparing two situations, a decentralized structure versus vertical integration indicates that the latter is more efficient not only for firms but also for consumers (the benefit of the integrated structure is greater than that of the decentralized structure, lower consumer prices). This is demonstrated below.

Profits of the Decentralized Structure

The Distributor It is assumed that the selling price to the consumer is the only strategic variable for the retailer:

$$max_p \Pi_{dis} = (p - p_w)(1 - p) \tag{5.2.3}$$

Deriving the Eq. (5.2.3), we have that $\frac{\delta \Pi}{\delta p} = 1 - 2p + p_w$. Therefore, $p^* = \frac{1+p_w}{2}$.

Replacing p^* in the demand (quantity) Eq. (5.2.4), we have that

$$D(p) = 1 - p = 1 - \left(\frac{1 + p_w}{2}\right) = q^* = \frac{1 - p_w}{2}. \tag{5.2.4}$$

So, by replacing p^* and q^* in the retailer's objective function (Eq. 5.2.3):

$$\Pi_{dis} = \left(\frac{1+p_w}{2} - p_w\right)\left(1 - \frac{1+p_w}{2}\right) = \left(\frac{1-p_w}{2}\right)^2.$$

The Producer Replacing $p^* = \frac{1+p_w}{2}$ in the Eq. (5.2.1), we have:

$$max\ p_w \Pi_{pro} = (p_w - c)(1-p) = (p_w - c)\left(\frac{1-p_w}{2}\right). \tag{5.2.5}$$

Differentiating equation (5.2.5), we obtain that $\frac{\delta \Pi}{\delta p_w} = 2 - 4p_w + 2c$. Therefore, $p_w^* = \frac{1+c}{2}$.

Replacing p_w^* in p^*, we have Eq. (5.2.6)

$$p^* = \frac{1+p_w}{2} = \frac{1+\frac{1+c}{2}}{2} = \frac{3+c}{4}. \tag{5.2.6}$$

The producer's profits are presented in Eq. (5.2.7):

$$\Pi_{pro} = (p_w - c)(1-p) = \left(\frac{1+c}{2} - c\right)\left(1 - \left(\frac{3+c}{4}\right)\right) = \frac{(1-c)^2}{8}, \tag{5.2.7}$$

and those of the distributor are presented in Eq. (5.2.8):

$$\Pi_{dis} = \left(\frac{1-p_w}{2}\right)^2 = \left(\frac{1-(\frac{1+c}{2})}{2}\right)^2 = \frac{(1-c)^2}{16}. \tag{5.2.8}$$

Therefore, the aggregation of the decentralized structure is (See Eq. (5.2.9)):

$$\Pi_{pro_dis} = \Pi_{pro} + \Pi_{dis} = \frac{(1-c)^2}{8} + \frac{(1-c)^2}{16} = \frac{3}{16}(1-c)^2. \tag{5.2.9}$$

Gains of the Centralized Structure

$$max_p \Pi_v = pq - cq = (p-c)(1-p) \tag{5.2.10}$$

Differentiating the Eq. (5.2.10), we obtain that $\frac{\delta\Pi_v}{\delta p} = 1 - 2p + c$. Therefore, the price of vertical integration is $p_v^* = \frac{1+c}{2}$.

The gains from vertical integration are the following Eq. (5.2.11):

$$\Pi_v = \left(\frac{1+c}{2} - c\right)\left(1 - \frac{1+c}{2}\right) = \frac{(1-c^2)}{4} \tag{5.2.11}$$

Therefore, $\Pi_v > \Pi_{prod_{is}}$ since

$$\frac{(1-c^2)}{4} > \frac{3}{16}(1-c)^2. \tag{5.2.12}$$

It is thus Eq. (5.2.12) demonstrated that the integrated structure is more efficient than the decentralized structure (chain monopolies), both from private and collective perspectives. This efficiency—reflected in higher overall profits and greater consumer surplus—stems from the elimination of the double marginalization problem.

Necessary Constraints It is shown that the outcomes of an integrated structure such as higher profits and lower consumer prices can be replicated without full integration by implementing vertical contractual constraints. These constraints, when properly designed, are sufficient to achieve the same level of efficiency and benefits as vertical integration.

To maximize joint benefits under double marginalization, the contract between the producer and the distributor must lead the distributor to choose the price of the integrated structure.

Three solutions are possible: a two-part tariff, an imposed resale price, and a *forcing*.

(i) **Two-Part Tariff** In the case of double marginalization, the distortion occurs because of the fact that the marginal cost of distribution differs from the marginal cost of the vertical structure.

To avoid this change, the producer price must be equal to the cost $p_w = c$. Therefore, the distribution firm is motivated to make the right decisions, that is, to choose the price of the integrated structure as the consumer price.

The two-part tariff includes a linear wholesale price equal to the producer marginal cost ($p_w = c$) and a fixed premium (A) that achieves the desired profit sharing.

The contract distributes the profits according to the distribution mode set in advance. To simplify, we can assume that the producer (principal) holds the bargaining power. In this case, the sharing method tries to give all the profits to the producer. To achieve this, the premium equals the profit of the integrated structure, whereas the retailer has zero profit.

Let the binomial tariff be:

$$T(q) = A + p_w q.$$

The retailer maximizes:

$$max_p (p - c)D(p) - A.$$

In this case, $p = p_i$, and the retailer's profit is equal to $\Pi_i - A$ where $\Pi_i = (p_i - c)D(p_i)$.

The wholesaler can appropriate the retailer's profits by imposing a franchise fee equal to the integrated structure's profit, i.e., $A = \Pi_i$. The retailer is said to be a "residual demander," that is, he receives all the marginal benefits.

In summary, we use two variables. The wholesale intermediary price ($p_w = c$) leads the distributor to choose $p = p_i$. The premium (A) allows the producer to capture the retailer's profit equal to the profit from vertical integration (Π_i).

(ii) **Imposed resale price or ceiling price** In this case, the producer determines the distributor's behavior by imposing the selling price on the consumer. This strategy prevents the retailer from behaving like a monopolist and forces him to behave as if he were under vertical integration. The producer chooses the wholesale price (pw) corresponding to the desired profit sharing. The producer sells to the intermediary at a good price $p_w = p_i$ and imposes a resale price $p = p_i$. Consequently, the retailer's profit is zero, and the producer obtains the benefit of the integrated structure (Π_i) since it sells to the retailer at a price that reaches the integration profit.

The ceiling price $p \leq \bar{p}$ leads to the same result. In summary, two variables are used, the wholesale intermediary price (p_w) and the resale price p, both of which are linked to the vertical integration price $p_w = p = p_i$.

(iii) Forcing It should be noted that "forcing," i.e., the minimum imposition by the intermediary of a wholesale quantity ($q \geq \underline{q}$), has the same effect as the resale price.

5.2.2 *The Distributor's Moral Hazard*

5.2.2.1 The problem

The theoretical framework is the moral hazard model presented in Sect. 5.1.4. The environment is deterministic, but the information asymmetry favors the agent (distributor).

In this case, we focus on distributor's effort when selling instead of the consumer price. This effort makes the product more attractive in the eyes of the consumer by incorporating elements such as free shipping, information before the sale, and advertising. Collectively, these components are referred to as the "promotional effort," which directly affects demand.

The producer is therefore interested in encouraging this effort. The simplest way would be to establish the level of effort required by the principal in the contract. However, this is not possible due to moral hazard, as the agent's effort cannot be accurately measured or observed.

In this new model, the final demand is of the form:

$q = D(p, s)$ where s is the promotional effort. It is assumed that $D'(p) < 0$ and that $D'(s) > 0$. Demand is decreasing relative to price and increasing relative to the promotional effort.

We also assume that only the retailer observes the cost of the promotional: $\Phi(s)$ is the cost of the promotional effort per unit, $\Phi'(s) > 0$; $q\Phi(s)$ is the total cost of this effort.

Centralized Structure Let p_i be the price of vertical integration and s_i be the service of vertical integration. p_i and s_i maximize in Eq. (5.2.13)

$$\Pi_i = [p - c - \Phi(s)]D(p, s). \tag{5.2.13}$$

Decentralized Structure

$$\Pi_m = (p_w - c)D(p, s)$$

$$\Pi_r = (p - p_w - \Phi(s))D(p, s)$$

The producer chooses $p_w > c$, since he is a monopolist.

In a second stage, the reseller maximizes his profits by choosing p and s.

We experience the problem of resale price distortion, where the retailer does not consider the wholesaler's profits associated with more services. Thus, there are two vertical externalities, one related to the choice of resale price and the other to choosing the level of promotional effort. The second externality is as follows:

$$(p_w - c)\frac{\delta D}{\delta s}$$

As before, this coordination problem occurs because producer's profits reduce retailer's profits in the vertical structure. Consequently, at a given resale price, the retailer offers too few services, which causes demand to fall.

5.2.2.2 *Necessary Constraints*

To encourage promotional efforts and gain the advantage of vertical integration, the producer can give the retailer residual demander status by choosing $p_w = c$. The wholesaler seizes the retailer's residual profit through a franchise fee $A = \Pi_i$.

Note that the imposed resale price is no longer sufficient. To fully capture the benefits of vertical integration, the producer must set the price $p = p_i$. However, the externality arises from the service provided, not just the price—making this equivalent to imposing a certain level of effort. Consequently, the producer's interest lies in combining resale price (or forcing) with additional mechanisms, such as requiring payment for advertising or other promotional efforts.

5.2.3 *The Case of a Retail Network*

The introduction of intra-brand competition, i.e., the wholesale industry is competitive. We focus on the problem of promotional efforts.

5.2.3.1 *The Problem*

A problem highlighted by Telser (1960) concerns the pre-sale service, i.e., documentation, testing, demonstration, etc. These services are essential for the sale of complex products (e.g., cars). Horizontal externality, i.e., between retailers, can be described as follows: a consumer takes advantage of the sales effort (information) of one retailer but ultimately buys the product from another retailer; thus, taking advantage of the free riding between retailers. Horizontal externality highlights a public good problem. The public good in a network is the information provided to consumers about the retailer's product. The result is a suboptimal level of the public good, i.e., insufficient sales effort.

This problem is illustrated by the following model, which represents the extreme case, where the service results in sales may not be captured by the retailer offering this effort.

Let $q = D(p, \bar{s})$ be the demand, $\bar{s}$ represent the maximum service for each retail network, and p be the lowest price charged by each retail network.

We assume that each consumer will initially get information from the retailer that offers the most complete information (i.e., the more comprehensive service). Then, at the second time, the consumer buys from the retailer with the lowest prices. $\Phi(s)$ represents the unit cost of the promotional effort for a consumer who visits the store but does not consume. It is assumed that $\Phi(s) = 0$.

A retailer offering a service $\bar{s}$ must achieve sufficient sales to offset the additional cost. At the same time, its resale price must not exceed the wholesale price of intermediaries due to intra-brand competition (a competitor could slightly reduce its sales prices and thus monopolize all demand when it does not provide the service). This scenario is for a service $\bar{s}$ with a resale price $p = p_w$. However,

$$p - [p_w + \Phi(\bar{s})] \leq 0.$$

Hence, $\bar{s} = 0$, i.e., no service is provided.

5.2.3.2 *Necessary Constraints*

The problem linked to horizontal externality and free riding between retailers comes from intra-brand competition. The solution to this problem is through the reduction of intra-brand competition: (i) imposed resale price, which guarantees the homogeneity of the network, preventing retailers from charging discounted prices that provide a sales effort, and (ii) territorial exclusivity, which ensures a geographic or retail monopoly that allows it to monopolize the results of its sales efforts.

5.2.4 Uncertainty and Risk Aversion of Retailers

We first define the causes of uncertainty in the producer-distributor relationship, before analyzing the impact on the two main vertical constraints under consideration (franchise rights, imposed sales price).

5.2.4.1 Uncertainty in the Producer-Distributor Relationship

There are two types of uncertainty: (i) uncertainty of demand resulting from variations in consumer tastes and the degree of inter-brand competition and (ii) uncertainty about the cost of distribution, i.e., the cost linked to technological progress, wages, etc.

The uncertainty hypothesis is introduced as follows: it is assumed to affect all retailers in the market uniformly. The analysis is structured into three distinct stages: (i) the signing of the contract in uncertainty; (ii) the uncertainty is resolved, and retailers acquire some information (level of final demand, cost of sale); and (iii) the retailers make decisions (choice of retail sale price, level of promotional effort) that affect the vertical structure. Therefore, the right to make decisions in response to environmental changes is delegated to the retailers.

5.2.4.2 Franchise Right in an Uncertain Environment

In an uncertain environment (when final demand and resale cost are random), the two-part tariff (residual claimant status) is still sufficient if the retailer is risk neutral.

Otherwise, if the retailer is risk averse, any increase in risk decreases the franchise fee that the producer can extract. This scenario highlights a key limitation of the franchise rights mechanism. Under the residual claimant status (linked to the two-part tariff), the retailer experiences excessive risk. The principal must arbitrate between incentives and insurance. Therefore, he will have to decrease the franchise fee and increase the wholesale price above marginal cost to (partly) insure the retailer. This scenario represents a risk-sharing contract.

5.2.4.3 Imposed Resale Prices Under Uncertainty

The agency problem is to design incentives that lead retailers to make decisions that closely resemble those made under vertical integration.

In an uncertain environment, the imposed resale price is not sufficient since it is set before uncertainty disappears. This constraint is insensitive to demand conditions and cost distribution.

The retailer's risk aversion exacerbates the problem since the imposed resale price makes the retailer bear all cost fluctuations that cannot be passed on to consumers. To support fluctuating demand for retailers, the contract must leave positive profits:

$p - p_w - y > 0$ and represents the unit cost of distribution.

In summary, the theoretical literature focusing on vertical coordination problems reveals that, in all cases, a simple linear tariff does not guarantee good coordination between a producer and its retailer (network) (s). The general lesson can be understood through competition policy: vertical restraints can eliminate double marginalization and free-riding problems.

5.2.5 *Review of the Literature on Franchise Networks*

In this section, the empirical evaluation of these results is based on the econometric literature on franchise networks.

A franchise agreement is a contract between two legally independent companies, whereby the franchisor grants the franchisee the right to operate under its brand and use its processes, production, and marketing methods in exchange for direct or indirect payments (Blair and Lafontaine 2005). These agreements are usually accompanied by a series of vertical restraints. It should be noted that only commercial franchises ("business format" franchise in US law), which are based on the rental of an intangible—the franchisor's brand—are legally defined at the European level.[6]

Franchise networks represent an ideal application scenario of contract theory (Pénard et al. 2004). Indeed, econometric tests of agency theory have been developed since the late 1980s (Brickley and Dark 1987; Norton 1988). The latter focused on the case of the United States.[7]

Most studies use a collection of information from several industries, but some econometric tests focus on one economic sector (fast-food industry:

[6] Article 1-3-b of Regulation 4087/88 of the European Community.

[7] In addition to commercial franchises, the law of The United States distinguishes between "traditional" franchising, in which the franchisor sells a final product to the franchisee for resale. The franchisor derives its income from the profits of the products sold to the franchisee (Lafontaine and Raynaud 2000). In commercial franchising, the franchisee is also a producer. With a few exceptions: Pénard et al. (2004) for France, Arruñada et al. (2001) and Vázquez (2004) for Spain, Pfister et al. (2006) covers nine countries.

Krueger 1991; Lafontaine and Kaufmann 1994; Kaufmann and Dant 1996; gas stations: A. Shepard 1993; Slade 1996; automobile industry: Arruñada et al. 2001).

An important empirical result is the evidence supporting the relevance of agency-related factors—such as cost control and moral hazard—in explaining the choice of organizational structure within wholesaler networks.

Agency costs would be decisive in the three problems identified by Pénard et al. (2004):

i The arbitrage between vertical integration versus delegation in the choice of the status of retailers, which constitutes a dominant theme of the econometric literature on franchise networks (Brickley and Dark 1987; Norton 1988; Minkler 1990; Lafontaine 1992a; Williams 1999).

ii The interest in dual distribution, i.e., mixed networks with own units and franchised units (Pénard et al. 2004).

iii The design of the contracts, i.e., the nature and content of the clauses that bind the franchisor and the franchisees. In this case, the contractual design is the main focus and not the choice of a network organization. As part of this problem, most works are dedicated to the study of the franchise as a distribution contract, i.e., the determination of the economic clauses: franchise fee and royalty rate (Norton 1988; Lafontaine 1992b; Minkler 1990).

5.3 To Remember

A contract is a reliable promise between two parties, in which the obligations of each are specified in an agreement.

The principal-agent paradigm deals with the bilateral or agency relationship where one of the parties contractually delegates (principal) to another (agent) an action or decision.

Contract economics includes three competing and complementary contract theories: (i) incentive theory (agency theory), (ii) transaction cost theory, and (iii) incomplete contract theory.

Information is the central point of the analysis of contract theory models.

5.4 Suggested Questions

1. An example of moral hazard is:

   a. An employee who works less than would be optimal for the employer because the employer cannot observe the employee's effort.
   b. An insurer who pays compensation to an insured who did not suffer a loss because the insurer cannot observe the probability that the insured will suffer a loss.
   c. A government who bails out a bank that is in financial trouble because the government cannot observe the bank's management.
   d. All of the above.

2. What is adverse selection?

   a. Process of selecting the best investment projects.
   b. Process where parties with asymmetric information select the least desirable outcomes.
   c. Process of eliminating risks in the market.
   d. Process of collective bargaining.

3. What is a signal in the information economy?

   a. A collusion agreement between companies.
   b. An action that reveals credible information to the other party.
   c. An outcome of perfect competition.
   d. A prediction of market behavior.

4. What is an incentive mechanism?

   a. A system that discourages competition.
   b. A system that aligns the interests of the parties involved through rewards or punishments.
   c. A system that eliminates information asymmetry.
   d. A system that ensures profit maximization.

5. What is uncertainty in economics?

   a. The certainty of an outcome.
   b. The lack of certainty about future outcomes.
   c. The complete availability of information.
   d. Perfect market predictability.

6. What is risk in economic terms?
   a. The probability of a negative event occurring.
   b. The absence of negative events.
   c. The certainty of a positive event.
   d. The predictability of market prices.
7. What is insurance in economics?
   a. An investment in the capital market.
   b. A contract to transfer risk from one party to another.
   c. A method of eliminating information asymmetry.
   d. A price agreement in a monopoly.
8. What is diversification in terms of investment?
   a. The concentration of investments in a single asset.
   b. The distribution of investments across several assets to reduce risk.
   c. The elimination of all risky investments.
   d. Investment only in government bonds.
9. What does risk aversion represent?
   a. The preference to avoid uncertainty and risk.
   b. The inclination to take high risks.
   c. Indifference to uncertainty.
   d. The pursuit of high-risk outcomes.
10. What is moral hazard?
    a. Risk assumed when investing in the capital market.
    b. Different behavior by a person when protected from the consequences.
    c. Risk due to changes in the interest rate.
    d. Risk related to inflation.

CHAPTER 6

Competition Policy

Competition policy is designed to bring markets closer to the social optimum—typically represented by perfect competition—where consumers retain all the economic surplus. It encompasses a set of laws aimed at guaranteeing competition. It is therefore a set of policies and laws aimed at guaranteeing competition. In this sense, the OECD 2007[1] defines competition policy as a process by which governments encourage competition and establish an enabling environment for it, by imposing or prohibiting certain business practices that may restrict it.

People often confuse competition policy with industrial policy. While competition policy seeks to preserve a competitive market and protect consumers, industrial policy has a more strategic and proactive approach, promoting specific sectors of the economy through incentives and regulations designed to strengthen their development. Industrial policy plays a crucial role in globalization contexts, where it faces the challenge of preventing the loss of strategic industrial capabilities through relocation processes. Furthermore, industrial policy promotes the maintenance of activities in the territory and the implementation and development of promising activities, such as industrial innovation agencies and competi-

[1] Organisation for Economic Co-operation and Development, founded in 1961, brings together 34 member countries, and its mission is to promote policies that improve the economic and social well-being of people around the world.

C. Lanchimba, *Industrial Organization*,
https://doi.org/10.1007/978-3-032-10906-4_6

tiveness hubs.[2] Unlike industrial policy, competition policy is the set of policies and laws designed to ensure that competition in a given market is not limited in a way that reduces economic welfare (Motta 2006). This objective translates into the monitoring of anticompetitive practices such as cartels, abuse of dominant position, and economic concentrations that may restrict market access or harm consumers. This definition recognizes the idea that companies can reduce competition in a way that is not harmful. To better understand this concept, let's analyze competition policy in the United States, Europe, and some Latin American countries.

6.1 Competition Policy in the United States

The origin of competition policy in the United States dates back to the nineteenth century; it was born as a set of measures applied in response to the development of *trusts*. A *trusts* is a large firm that buys smaller companies to limit competition and gain market momentum. In the capitalist societies of the nineteenth century, *trusts* played an important economic role. Thus, *trusts* and cartels occur when several small companies join forces to gain market power. Two types of concentrations can induce *trust*: horizontal concentration, which is the acquisition of companies in the same sector, and vertical concentration, which involves the acquisition of the entire production chain from raw materials to the finished product. In this context, the Sherman Act was enacted.

6.1.1 The Sherman Act

This law was adopted in 1889 and is the starting point of competition policy. During the second part of the nineteenth century, the manufacturing industry in the United States experienced significant changes, including the development of means of transport and communication (railroad, telephone, telegraph). These changes brought about the formation of a large integrated market and the incitement of companies to achieve economies of scale, leading to increased competition, i.e., it was a period of low and unstable prices. Consequently, a price war took place, maintained

[2] A set of small, medium, and large companies, research laboratories, and training institutions, grouped with a specific objective in a given territory (Délégation interministérielle á l'aménagement du territoire et á l'attractivité régionale, Francia, 2014).

by companies to recover their large investments related to research and economies of scale. In this context, companies were tempted to make agreements on prices to maintain high prices, which is precisely the purpose of the organization of cartels and *trusts.*

In turn, this situation negatively impacted consumers and companies that used inputs produced by cartels and *trusts.* Small companies complained about the unfair trade practices of their competitors.

In many US states, small businesses harmed by cartels and trusts had sufficient political influence to drive the adoption of antitrust legislation. However, the laws could do little against the agreements in several states. Soon, a consensus was reached to create a Federal Law that was approved in 1889, the so-called Sherman Act, which in its two main sections states:

Section 1 *Every contract, combination in the form of monopoly or otherwise, in restraint of agreements or trade ... is hereby declared unlawful*, i.e., it prohibits contracts and agreements that restrict competition.

Section 2 *Any person who monopolizes or attempts to monopolize, or combines or conspires with any person or persons, to monopolize any part of trade or commerce ... shall be deemed guilty of a felony* ..., i.e., it prohibits monopolization and attempts to monopolize. However, a monopoly is not illegal per se; what is punishable is the abuse of a dominant market position (prices far above marginal cost).

Indeed, the law allows for exceptions, particularly through the distinction between conduct deemed *per se* illegal *a*nd that evaluated under the *rule of reason.* If a practice turns out to be *illegal per se*, no argument can justify it, that is, the practice is prohibited without exception. Price agreement between competing companies is an example that illustrates this situation. On the contrary, in the case of a practice prohibited by a rule *rule of reason,*[3] a company can convince the Court of Justice that in this case the practice does not affect welfare (rule of reason).

On the other hand, the Sherman Act does not cover mergers between companies. Therefore, other complementary laws were created such as the Clayton Act and the Federal Trade Commission Act.

[3] The *rule of reason* is based on the principle of economic equilibrium: balance, costs, and benefits of each operation.

6.1.2 Clayton Act and the Federal Trade Commission Act

The Clayton Act was introduced in 1914 to extend antitrust legislation to mergers, as they also reduce competition. Since its implementation, this law has undergone several modifications (amendments). On the other hand, the Federal Trade Commission Act, enacted in 1914, addresses unfair methods of competition and deceptive trade practices.

After the war and until the 1970s, there was a period of intense antitrust activity. This period was characterized by the desire to limit large companies, rather than by the goal of achieving economic efficiency. Many economists at the University of Chicago strongly criticized the interventionist approach of antitrust authorities and the judiciary. This perspective began to influence judges and commentators in the 1970s.

This new trend brought about a significant shift during the Reagan era, as market forces were allowed to select the most efficient companies. This policy change was reinforced by other theoretical elements, such as the theory of contestable markets, i.e., a focus on economic efficiency.

Competition policy in the United States reflects the political power and influence of two schools of thought, Harvard (hardening, SCP) and Chicago (liberal economists focusing on economic efficiency). In short, these laws prohibit explicit agreements that aim to reduce the intensity of competition. Later, competition policy was implemented in Europe.

An example of the application of this law is the case of Microsoft. Microsoft was accused of abusing its dominant position by selling computers with its own operating system preinstalled, including web browsers, thus limiting consumer choice. The providers of other web browsers such as Opera, Native Tor, and Netscape accused Microsoft of restricting competition because they had to be purchased in stores or downloaded separately, often with slower speeds and greater difficulty. In 1999, it was determined that Microsoft committed monopolization and attempted monopolization by taking deliberate steps to suppress major competitors such as Apple, Java, and Netscape, among others (Liebowitz and Margolis 2001).

6.2 Competition Policy in Europe

Competition policy in the European Union developed later in the United States. The objective of this competition policy is to ensure fair competition among companies that provide consumers with a variety of choices and lower prices for high-quality products through innovation.

The institutions that make up the European Union and competition policy in Europe are the following: the Competition Legislation in Force, the European Council, the Council of the European Union, the European Parliament, the Court of Auditors, the Court of Justice of the European Union, the European Commission, the European Central Bank, and the European Economic and Social Committee (European Commission 2019b). There are two levels of courts in the European Union: the national and the European. Thus, the most interesting to study is the European level, since national competition policies are generally recent.

The European Commission implemented competition policy in the European Union, following the Treaty of Rome model and taking the Treaty of Paris as its starting point. It has investigative powers and imposes sanctions on anticompetitive practices.

The *Treaty of Paris* is a series of measures adopted by the six founding countries in 1951, which created the ECSC.[4] This treaty prohibits trade barriers and discriminatory and restrictive practices affecting competition. Two main reasons justified the introduction of competition policy measures in the treaty: (i) the desire to avoid the dangers of German domination and (ii) the preference for a functioning free market over a centralized one.

On the other hand, the *Treaty of Rome* is a new enumeration of the European treaties within the framework of the *Treaty of Amsterdam* that entered into force on May 1, 1999. These were established based on Articles 101 and 102 of the Treaty that established the the European Union (TFEU), which were previously Articles 81 and 82 of the Treaty establishing the European Community (ECT), which were in turn Articles 85 and 86 of the Treaty of Rome. These articles are characterized by "direct application," that is, these elements are part of the legislation of each Member State and can be applied directly by national courts. These articles apply at two levels: the European level and the national level by the competition authorities of each state.

[4] European Coal and Steel Community. It was a supranational entity at the European level that regulated the coal and steel sectors of the Member States: France, West Germany, Italy, Belgium, Luxembourg, and the Netherlands.

Article 101 TFEU (formerly 81 ECT and 85 of the Treaty of Rome) states the following: *It is prohibited ...: (a) to fix, directly or indirectly, the purchase or sale prices of ... (b) to limit or control production ... (c) to share out markets or sources of supply ..., (d) to apply to third parties unequal conditions for equivalent services ..., (e) to conclude contracts subject to the acceptance by the other parties of additional services ...*. In other words, it prohibits horizontal and vertical agreements. The nature of agreements between companies may affect trade between Member States, causing a restriction or distortion of competition. It also includes the conditions for direct and indirect sales, such as the price.

However, this prohibition does not apply when there are expectations of enhanced production and distribution of goods, technical and economic progress while guaranteeing consumers an equitable share of the benefits. On the other hand, Article 101 deals with both horizontal and vertical agreements. This is problematic for economic analysis because it assumes that these two categories of agreements have the same impact on competition.

In general, horizontal agreements are alliances between competitors that restrict competition and thus reduce the consumers' welfare. These agreements should be prohibited, except in very special cases, such as agreements for cooperation in research and development.

Conversely, vertical agreements occur between companies at different stages of the production process, generally favoring economic efficiency. This market structure creates problems if one company has significant market power, that is, when there is an underlying issue of horizontal market concentration.

Consequently, agreements that have different effects on competition are dealt with by the same legal clause. Recently, the European Community has understood and adopted an approach to vertical restraints that is more in line with economic thinking.

Controls are usually applied to markets characterized by a high level of concentration. Particularly, companies must report their potential role to competition authorities to assess the effect of this merger on future competition. The objective, following *Article 101*, is to prevent companies from merging to create or reinforce market power. To do this and determine whether the merger could have anticompetitive effects, the authorities will measure aspects such as the degree of concentration of supply, potential demand, barriers to entry, and potential competition, among others.

In some cases, the merger is permitted without further objection. However, in others, the authorities carry out an economic assessment to determine whether the merger can have positive effects in terms of efficiency or economic progress, such as the creation of new services, improved product quality, cost savings, or job preservations. Therefore, if the positive effects are significant, the merger is permitted. A clear example of the potential benefits of a merger is the case in France involving Darty, a household appliance retailer, and the Fnac group, an electronics retailer, which proposed to acquire Darty. The rationale behind the merger was that, although both companies operated in the retail electronics sector, they specialized in different product categories. Therefore, a merger would improve their efficiency and competitiveness, even at an international level, as their main competitor would be Amazon. The competition authority permitted this merger after a year of analysis, setting as a condition that six stores in Paris must be sold.

Article 102 of the TFEU of the ECT (formerly article 82 of the ECT and 86 of the Treaty of Rome) specifies the abuse of a dominant position. An abusive practice is defined as follows: "*(a) directly or indirectly imposing purchase or sale prices…, (b) limiting production…, (c) applying unequal conditions to third-party contractors for equivalent services…, (d) subordinating the conclusion of contracts to the acceptance, by the other contractors, of supplementary services….*"

Until 1990, EU authorities monitored agreements and abuse of dominant position based on Articles 85 and 86 of the Treaty of Rome. Since September 1, 1990, the regulation on the control of concentrations has been in force.

Concentration operations may occur either through the merger of initially independent companies or through the acquisition of control, such as the purchase of assets or contractual agreements.

Concentration operations may occur either through the merger of initially independent companies or through the acquisition of control, such as the purchase of assets or contractual agreements.

The implementation of competition policy in the European Union has produced significant results. For instance, according to the European Commission (2014), fines imposed on cartels in 2013 amounted to between $4,890 and $5,660 million. These revenues were allocated to the general budget of the European Union, thereby reducing the financial contributions required from Member States. In fact, the penalties for those who break these laws are up to 10% of the firm's worldwide turnover, plus

Table 6.1 Summary of sections of antitrust laws in Europe and the United States. Source: Author

Agreements	Article 101 TFEU Sherman Act Sec. 1 + Clayton Act Sec. 3
Abuse of dominant position Sherman Act Sec. 2 +	Article 102 TFEU Clayton Act Sec. 2
Control of concentrations	Regulation 139/2004 Clayton Act Sec. 7 + others
State aid	Article 107 TFEU

the prison sentences that producers can receive. A particular example of this application was the fine of 1,470 million Euros to the cartel formed by producers of tubes for computer and television screens. This cartel was in force for two decades. Asian producers exchanged information on screen dimensions and computer applications and agreed on the price between 2001 and 2006. This collusion harmed European consumers because most of these products came from Asia.

In short, the objective of competition policy is to ensure that firms compete fairly, allowing consumers to benefit from greater choice, better quality, and fair prices. Similarly, the European Commission encourages competition globally. However, within its treaty, state aid is prohibited with justified exceptions.

In this context, Article 103 TFEU (formerly Article 83 TEC) establishes that a committee shall adopt the measures necessary for the proper application of Articles 101 and 102 TFEU after consulting the European Parliament. The functions of the Commission and the Court of Justice of the European Union are also defined.

The instruments of competition policy can be summarized as follows:

Below is Table 6.1 based on Table 6.2, which shows the sanctions that some companies have suffered. We can see that the sanctions can be very severe if the company is found guilty.

6.2.1 *Cartels and Public Policies*

In the nineteenth century, cartels were common and legal in the United States (steel, sugar, oil, etc.). In France, since 1810, Article 419 of the Penal

Table 6.2 Summary of sanctions and companies. Source: Author

Year	Companies	Agreements	Infringement	Resolution	Article
2020	United States vs Google (Rosen 2024)	Abuse of dominant position	Illegally maintaining monopolies over search and search advertising	No sanction has yet been issued and the case is ongoing	Sherman Act Sec. 2. Clayton Act Sec. 2
2017	European Commission vs Google Shopping (Moreno 2021)	Abuse of dominant position	Abusing its dominant position in the market for general online search services, favoring its shopping service	Google paid 2.4 billion as a fine for the infringement (Corte Suprema Comisión Europea 2021)	Article 102 TFEU. Article 54 of the EEA
2019	Siemens AG (Germany) and Alstom S. A. (France) (Posada 2024)	Merger control	Merging their rail transport businesses through the purchase of shares	Prohibited the integration on insufficient and inadequate grounds	Regulation 139/2004
2011	AT&T and Time Warner (DOJ 2019)	Merger control	Merge both companies in the mobile phone market	The government's request to block the $85 billion merger was denied (Cornestone Research 2019)	Clayton Act Sec. 2
2017	Banca "Monti dei Paschi di Siena" and the Italian government (Corte Suprema di cassazione 2019)	State aid	The Italian government granted state aid to the bank, which was in financial difficulties at the time	The Commission approved aid under certain conditions to avoid distorting competition in the financial market	Article 107 of the TFEU
2016	Apple and the Irish government (Court of Justice of the European Union. 2024)	State aid	Apple had been receiving tax aid in the form of unpaid taxes from the Irish government since 1991	The European Commission ordered Ireland to recover approximately $14.5 billion in unpaid taxes from Apple (Ray 2024)	Article 107 TFEU

Code has prohibited agreements that aim to fix prices "above or below what free and natural competition would have determined." However, in practice, courts punish other cases as well. As noted, in the late nineteenth and early twentieth centuries, the US Congress passed two laws against high prices charged by "*trusts*" through the Sherman Antitrust Act of 1890 and the Federal Trade Commission Act of 1914. Similarly, in Europe, Article 81 of the ECT prohibits cartels.

According to OECD (2000), some examples of sanctions for agreements are the following:

- *Global Graphite Electrode Cartel*: $300 million and prison sentences in the United States; €218 million in Europe
- *Global Vitamin Agreements*: $1 billion and prison sentences in the United States; €855 million in Europe
- *Global Agreements on the Lysine*[5] *and citric acid*: $ 200 million and prison sentences in the United States

The severity of the prohibition on cartels depends on the country (in the United States, they are usually stricter). The interpretation of what constitutes an agreement can also vary between countries (ambiguity). This list can include agreements for research and development, professional associations, and the exchange of information.

On the other hand, the laws include leniency programs, which were introduced in the United States and Europe in 1993 and 2002, respectively. This program puts cartel members in a prisoner's dilemma situation since the objective of this program is to destabilize the structure. In fact, a participant in a cartel can denounce the existence of the cartel to enjoy a partial or total reduction of sanctions. Currently, in Europe, firms that engage in collusive behavior can be fined up to 10% of their annual revenues.

In cases handled by the US Department of Justice (DOJ) between 1963 and 1972, agreements between firms were most likely to occur when the number of market participants was small: 48% of these agreements were between 6 firms or less, 6.5% were between only 50 or more firms, and the average number of firms was 7.25 participants. In cartel cases between 1990 and 2003, 77% involved agreements among 6 or fewer firms, while only 13% involved agreements among 50 or more firms.

[5] It is an amino acid that is a component of proteins synthesized by living beings.

Indeed, both theoretical and empirical work show that more concentrated markets are more prone to collusion, as they facilitate closer monitoring of cartel members' behavior and enable earlier detection of potential issues. Companies can also reinforce the collusive nature of the market by increasing entry barriers. Large companies can acquire small firms to increase market concentration and eliminate those unwilling to integrate into their structure.

An interesting case of sanctions on the context of cartels occurred in 2019, where a cartel based on a restriction on technical development and not on price fixing or market share distribution was sanctioned for the first time. The European Commission sanctioned Daimler, BMW, and the Volkswagen Group (Volkswagen, Audi, and Porsche), because regular technical meetings were held, over more than 5 years, reaching an agreement to avoid competing on emission-cleaning technologies beyond what was legally required, despite having the technological capacity to do so. The Commission imposed a fine of €502,362,000 on the Volkswagen Group and €372,827,000 on BMW.

Daimler has not been fined, as it disclosed the existence of the cartel to the Commission. Moreover, it is important to highlight that all parties acknowledged their participation in the cartel and agreed to settle the case (The European Commission 2021; CentroCompetencia (CeCo) 2021). Particularly, Daimler, BMW, and the Volkswagen Group reached an agreement on AdBlue tank sizes and ranges and a common understanding on the estimated average AdBlue consumption. They also exchanged sensitive commercial information on these elements. In this way, they removed uncertainty about their future behavior on the market regarding emissions cleaning not beyond legal requirements (so-called overcompliance) and AdBlue refill ranges.

6.3 Competition Policy in Latin America

6.3.1 Argentina

Competition policy in Argentina dates to 1923 and was inspired by the US Sherman Act, with the first two articles of the Argentine law closely resembling those of the American legislation. This law was replaced in 1946, the first article prohibiting the creation or maintenance of monopolies and the second a listing concerted practices by companies. These laws were enforced primarily through criminal sanctions, and between 1933 and

1980, companies that violated them were penalized on only four occasions. Subsequently, in 1980, law 22.2262 was passed. Its articles were based on Articles 85 and 86 of the Treaty of Rome. Finally, the modern version of Law 25.156 was enacted in 1999, which included control over mergers and the creation of the National Court for the Defense of Competition. However, the latter was never established. This law for the defense of competition penalized exclusively acts and conduct, not market structures.

For the implementation of this law, the National Commission for the Defense of Competition (CNDC) was established, along with a proposed tribunal composed of seven members. However, this tribunal lacked the necessary authority. As a result, the CNDC functions in an advisory capacity, while regulatory decisions are made by the Secretariat of Technical Coordination—previously known as the Secretariat of Competition, Deregulation, and Consumer Protection.

One of the well-known cases of the application of this law was that of the cartel formed by six cement producers, which operated for 20 years. These companies exchanged information on production, distribution, and sales. Five of the six companies from this cartel were fined several millions, while the other lost market share as a penalty for attempting to leave the cartel (OECD 2007).

6.3.2 *Brazil*

Currently, the country's competition law (Sistema Brasileiro de Defesa da Concorrência, SBDC) is made up of three bodies: the Administrative Council for Economic Defense (CADE) that adjudicates the cases, the Secretariat of Economic Law (SDE) that oversees the investigation, and the Secretariat of Economic Monitoring of the Ministry of Finance, which is responsible for the economic analysis of the processes.

This law emerged in the aftermath of the Second World War, during a period marked by significant government intervention in the market. It controlled the prices of most sectors, as well as industries, the financial field, and transportation. Given the lack of market freedom, the Competition Law was created in 1962 by CADE. Subsequently, in 1994, after the period of hyperinflation and the adoption of the real as the exchange rate, strong fiscal and credit policies were introduced. Likewise, laws were introduced to control mergers. During this period, most state-owned companies were privatized (OECD 2007).

Brazilian competition policy defines laws such as Article 173, which prohibits the abuse of economic power, the elimination of competition, and arbitrary increase in profits.

Similarly, it promotes free enterprise, competition, and consumer protection. Moreover, Brazilian law prohibits mergers, horizontal and vertical agreements, as well as abuses of market power.

6.3.3 Ecuador

Ecuador's Anti-monopoly Law, officially known as the Organic Law for the Regulation and Control of Market Power, is relatively recent—enacted in 2011—and includes specific provisions aimed at controlling market dominance. This law was established later than in other Latin American countries. In this region, the first country to have an Anti-monopoly Law was Argentina (1923), followed by Colombia (1953) and Chile (1973). Currently, almost all Latin American countries have some legislation of this type.

The Organic Law of Regulation and Control of Market Power in Ecuador shows significant similarities with the legislation of countries such as the United States, Mexico, Chile, Argentina, and Colombia. The objective of this law is framed in *Article 1*, which regulates "the promotion of the interests of both suppliers and consumers to participate in markets free of obstacles, fostering better prices and broader options through the control, prevention, correction, prohibition, elimination, and sanction - where applicable - of the abuse of economic operators with market power, collusive agreements, economic concentration operations, and other restrictive and unfair practices" (República del Ecuador 2011). In this article, we can distinguish that the sections on abuse of dominant position and agreements, presented in Table 6.1, are framed.

Despite the law's relatively short existence, 227 investigations were conducted between 2013 and 2017, resulting in eight sanctions. This outcome suggests that, under antitrust law, companies have become more rigorous in meeting the same regulatory requirements.

6.4 Concentration and Market Power

After studying the importance of competition policy and addressing central points such as concentration and market power, it is necessary to define these concepts in more depth. Therefore, we begin by examining market power, followed by the definition of the relevant market, and conclude with a discussion on market concentrations.

6.4.1 Market Power

A firm can increase its price above its marginal cost, that is, the price of perfect competition. Market power is usually measured by the Lerner Index (6.4.3). The development of this Index is presented below,

$$\pi_i = p(q_i)q_i - c_i, \tag{6.4.1}$$

where π_i is the profit of firm i, $p(q_i)$ is the market price that depends on the total quantity supplied, q_i is the quantity supplied by firm i, and c_i is the total production cost of firm i.

$$\frac{\delta \pi_i}{\delta q_i} = \left[p + \frac{\delta p}{\delta q_i} q_i\right] - MC_i = 0 \tag{6.4.2}$$

$$MC_i = p\left[1 + \frac{1}{\frac{\delta q_i/q_i}{\delta p/p}}\right]$$

where MC_i is the marginal cost of firm i; the price elasticity of demand is $e_q = \frac{\delta q_i/q_i}{\delta p/p}$. Rearranging equation (6.4.2), we have that:

$$L = \frac{p_i - MC_i}{p_i} = -\frac{1}{e_q}. \tag{6.4.3}$$

The more inelastic the demand (low price sensitivity) is, the greater the firm's market share becomes. The Lerner Index (6.4.3) takes values between 0 and 1. In a market, the greater the power of the firms, the more their behavior will resemble that of a monopoly, acting as if they were the sole producers. Conversely, if the market is competitive, this index will be equal to 0.

Excessive market power is a problem when the price is raised well above marginal cost, as this reduces consumer welfare. Certain practices that a firm with excess market power may also engage in are tied sales.[6] These types of practices are illegal from the perspective of competition policy. Other sources of power that can be mentioned are the following: inelastic demand for certain goods, economies of scale, barriers to entry, the ability of companies to coordinate their strategies (cartel), product differentiation, etc.

Due to the difficulty of using the Eq. (6.4.3) to measure market power, we can estimate it through other tools presented below. However, it is necessary to first define the relevant market (*relevant market*). To do this process, we must answer two questions:

Product market: What products should be included in the market?
Geographic market: What geographic area should be considered?

In this context, we define *market* as a set of products that are highly substitutable from a supply and demand perspective.

6.4.2 Definition of Relevant Market

The European Commission (2019a) defines the relevant market in terms of products, including all goods or services that consumers regard as interchangeable or substitutable based on their characteristics, prices, or intended use.

We distinguish between two types of substitution: demand-side substitution, where consumers view products as interchangeable, and supply-side substitution, where producers of other goods could feasibly switch to producing the product in question if its price rises (an example of this type of substitution occurred at the start of the pandemic, when companies traditionally producing goods like paint shifted their operations to manufacture alcohol-based sanitizers in response to rising demand and prices). Below is an example of substitutability of supply and demand:

Example 6.3 (Different Quality Paper) In the case of paper, there are several markets because the differences in qualities range from low to high from the perspective of demand.

[6] Or subordinate or joint sales, which consists of offering or selling several products in the same batch without offering these products separately at the same price.

Example 6.4 (Demand Substitutability) In the case of smartphones, consumer preferences between brands are influenced by structural factors such as product features, brand reputation, pricing, and social influence (Suki 2013).

Example 6.5 (Nestlé/Perrier Merger (1992)) What is a relevant market? Does mineral water belong to the same market as sugary soft drinks (soft drinks)? In this case, there is no demand substitutability because the needs and characteristics are different. On the other hand, there is supply substitutability, as there are no significant or specific barriers preventing mineral water companies from entering the soft drinks market.

Example 6.6 (Regarding Supply-Side Substitutability) In the case of JK Tyre and Industries Ltd, it was determined that tire manufacturers could readily switch production between different types of vehicle tires. As a result, the Commission considered supply-side substitutability when assessing competition in the tire market (Soni 2024).

One of the mechanisms to determine the relevant market is also the cross-elasticity of demand.

Cross-Elasticity of Demand
Cross-elasticity of demand (Eq. 6.4.4) measures the percentage change in demand for one product in response to a change in the price of another product.

$$\epsilon_{a,b} = \frac{\delta Q_a}{\delta P_b} \frac{P_b}{Q_a} \tag{6.4.4}$$

When small changes in the price of the product b lead to significant changes in the demand for product a, the product is said to be elastic. Otherwise, it is inelastic. For example, when the price of rice rises, people prefer potatoes.

Set of Signals

In parallel with the use of cross-elasticity of demand, competition authorities employ a set of tests to demonstrate the relevance of a product within a market. The tests can be the following:

1. **Price correlation over time**: For example, a high correlation (between 0.85 and 1) observed between the prices of mineral water and sugary soft drinks may suggest substitutability.
2. **Price differences**: Significant and persistent price gaps between sugary soft drinks and mineral water can indicate that they belong to distinct markets.
3. **Nature of the need satisfied**: For example, the distinction between cosmetics sold in pharmacies versus those sold in supermarkets may reflect different consumer needs or perceptions, suggesting separate market segments.
4. **Geographic market**: The role of imports and transport costs is considered in many industries like mineral water. For many, France is a geographic market because there is little trade with other European states. Furthermore, the transport cost for mineral water is high relative to the value of the good. Finally, entry into the French market is difficult, as it is a mature market and there are well-established brands.

With the elements presented, the competition authority could determine the relevant market in which a product should be present. After defining the market, the authority can determine whether there is market power; for this purpose, it defines a measure of market power such as the Lener Index. It also examines whether specific market characteristics—such as high levels of concentration—contribute to the existence or persistence of market power.

6.4.3 *Market Concentration*

There are markets where the number of firms is large, and the market share of each firm is small. There are also markets where the opposite situation prevails: there are few firms, and each firm's market is large. In other markets, one or more firms control a large market share, while other firms have a very small part of that market. These differences in market share affect competitiveness.

Market concentration can increase either when certain firms grow more rapidly than their competitors or because of mergers and acquisitions within the market.

6.4.3.1 *Defining Concentration*

Defining concentration is necessary for the following reasons: (i) to determine the extent of the market concentration and (ii) to compare the market in question with others from the perspective of concentration. An accurate measurement of concentration is also important for competition regulators.

When there is more than one firm in an economic sector, two factors influence concentration: the number of firms in sector and the distribution of market shares among firms.

The total amount produced by the industry is as follows: $Q = \sum_{i=1}^{N} q_i$ where N is the number of firms in the industry, Q is the aggregate output level (the quantity sold to consumers), and q_i is the quantity produced by firm i, $i = 1, 2 \ldots, N$.

Likewise, s_i is the market share of firm i, given by $s_i = \frac{q_i}{Q} * 100$, i.e., it is the percentage of industry sales made by firm i. Additionally, we have that $0 \leq s_i \leq 100$ and $\sum_{i=1}^{N} s_i = 100$.

6.4.3.2 *Measures of Concentration*

Below are two commonly used concentration measures, particularly by the US Federal Trade Commission to analyze a potential merger of two companies.

Top Four Concentration Ratio (I4)

This ratio is calculated by adding up the market shares of the top four companies from 1 to N in descending order of market share.

The ratio is then:

$$I_4 = \sum_{i=1}^{4} s_i.$$

Table 6.3 shows that using the I_4 index can be problematic, as we conclude that industries 1 and 2 exhibit a similar market concentration even though they are different. For instance, in industry 1, one firm has 65% of the market, while in industry 2, no firm exceeds 20%.

Table 6.3 Example of concentration ratio of the first four companies. Source: Author

Market Sh %	s1	s2	s3	s4	s5	s6	s7	s8	s9	s10	I4
Industry 1	65	5	5	5	5	5	5	5	5	5	80
Industry 2	20	20	20	20	0	0	0	0	0	0	80
Industry 3	100/3	100/3	100/3	0	0	0	0	0	0	0	100
Industry 4	49	49	1/4	1/4	1/4	1/4	1/4	1/4	1/4	1/4	98.5

Table 6.4 Example of Herfindahl-Hirschman Index. Source: Author

Market Sh %	s1	s2	s3	s4	s5	s6	s7	s8	s9	s10	HHI
Industry 1	65	5	5	5	5	5	5	5	5	5	3850
Industry 2	20	20	20	20	0	0	0	0	0	0	2000
Industry 3	100/3	100/3	100/3	0	0	0	0	0	0	0	3333
Industry 4	49	49	1/4	1/4	1/4	1/4	1/4	1/4	1/4	1/4	4802

Herfindahl-Hirschman Index I_{HH}
This index is a convex function of the market share, given by the following expression:

$$I_{HH} = \sum_{i=1}^{n} (s_i)^2$$

I_{HH} is more sensitive to unequal market shares. Thus, Table 6.4 shows that the concentration of industry 1 is almost twice as high as that of industry 2.

We can observe in Table 6.3 that industries 3 and 4 have similar levels of concentration. However, in Table 6.4, it is observed that industry 4 is more concentrated.

6.4.4 *Mergers*

Mergers between companies in the same market increase the concentration of that market. Mergers refer to the purchase, acquisition, or integration of independent companies into a single entity.

Mergers can lead to cost reductions, thereby enhancing a company's efficiency. They can also allow companies to combine their specific characteristics and increase their capacity for innovation. On the other hand, they can provide quick access to new geographic markets. They also reduce competition and increase the market power of the merging companies. In this sense, companies analyze the benefits of the merger in terms of reduction and innovation. If a merger is not profitable, firms prefer not to carry it out. These mergers can be classified into three categories:

Horizontal Merger The two companies that merge produce the same product or similar products and sell this product in the same market. Example: Formed in 1999, the Renault-Nissan alliance brought together two major car manufacturers. By 2003, the group operated in over 200 countries and today ranks as the fourth-largest automobile manufacturer in the world. They operate under a cross-shareholder model. According to official figures from the company, Renault has 42.43% of Nissan's capital, while Nissan has 15% of Renault. By 2014, the key areas of the merger include engineering, manufacturing, and logistics, as well as purchasing and human resources (Groupe Reault 2016). Another example is the 2020 merger between T-Mobile and Sprint, valued at $30 billion. Both companies operated in the mobile telephony and wireless services sector, and the merged entity now operates under the T-Mobile name. This merger aims to accelerate the progress and modernization of wireless technology, forging the 5G network to transform mobile telephony, drive innovation, and offer new experiences to customers (T-Mobile 2020; Lee 2020).

Vertical Merger A firm producing intermediate goods or inputs of production merges with a firm that uses those goods to produce final goods. Firms pursue this type of merger because it facilitates coordination and reduces management costs. Example: Balan et al. (2015) point out that the proposed acquisition of EagleView Technology Corp by Verisk Analytics, Inc., is a vertical merger problem since both companies provide complementary inputs. EagleView offers products for the insurance industry to calculate the dimensions of building roofs used to determine the costs of repairing or replacing roofs. Verisk Analytics, Inc. uses its databases and industry experience to provide predictive analytics and decision support solutions, data management, etc. However, these firms could not merge as the US Federal Trade Commission (FTC) determined that the deal was problematic because it would combine the only two notable competitors that offered aerial measurement products used by the insurance industry to calculate the dimensions of building roofs. Therefore, the merger problem would also be horizontal. Finally, Verisk Analytics, Inc. withdrew from a proposed USD 650 million acquisition deal with EagleView due to the difficulties of this merger. The FTC argued that this merger could lead to higher prices for insurance companies and consumers.

Another example of this type of merger is Facebook's acquisition of WhatsApp in 2014 for a total of $ 19 billion, marking the largest social media acquisition to date. For Facebook, this is a key growth area because even if they don't monetize this product, it is a way to attract the next billion smartphone consumers into their ecosystem and interact with them (BBC News 2014).

Conglomerate Merger Some companies that produce different goods merge. In many cases, the interest lies in sharing management services, distribution, etc. We distinguish three cases of conglomeration:

1. **Product extension**: The companies involved in the merger are functionally connected through stages of production or distribution. A conglomeration in product extension is the merger of personal care companies in the United States. In 2005, Procter & Gamble Company acquired control of the entirety of The Gillette Company (Gillette, USA) through a share purchase. The merger created the largest personal care and shaving products company in the world. Furthermore, this acquisition allowed the company to diversify its product portfolio, resulting in an increased average net profit margin of 13.6% in the post-merger period (Kumar 2019).
2. **Market extension**: The companies involved in the merger produce targeted products, but each company operates in different markets geographically. An example of this is Amazon, which acquired physical establishments and bought Whole Foods Market, a gourmet organic food chain, for $ 13.7 billion on August 24, 2017, to expand its grocery business. This merger allowed Amazon to enter a new market, turning it into a company that sells any type of product (Cain 2022).
3. **Other conglomerates**: There is no relationship between the companies that merge. An example of a merger of other conglomerates is Matheson Gardens, based in Hong Kong, which encompasses a diverse group of companies, including Jardine Pacific, Jardine Motors, Hongkong Land, Dairy Farm, Mandarin Oriental, and Jardine Cycle &

Carriage, among others. The operations of this conglomerate focus on Asia. In 2013, they were among the top 200 publicly traded companies.

There are several reasons for mergers, including reducing competition, saving money, gaining prestige for the manager, and capitalizing on the low market valuation of the target company, among others. We might think that by reducing competition, a merger within an industry would have little noticeable impact on consumers and overall social welfare. A merger can have positive and negative effects on social welfare.

Mergers have a positive effect on production because the least efficient company in the market stops producing. On the contrary, a merger can negatively impact consumers if it leads to a monopoly, as the dominant firm may exploit its market power to raise prices, thereby reducing consumer welfare.

Finally, market concentration can be the result of the existence of market entry barriers.

6.4.4.1 Barriers to Entry

In several industries, there is little or no entry of new companies, and the companies in that market earn profits. This phenomenon can be attributed to the presence of entry barriers in the industry-strategic actions by incumbent firms aimed at deterring potential competitors.

Consequently, a company's market power is limited not only by the presence of other companies but also by the potential companies that can enter the market.

An example of barriers to entry is the pharmaceutical market, where companies seeking to enter the market have some restrictive barriers related to state policy, such as licenses, drug registration, examinations, and drug certification (Shuvanova and Rohulia 1942). Additionally, the market faces barriers due to competition from several recognized pharmaceutical companies, making it challenging for new brands to enter the market.

According to Bain (1956), several factors may play a role in its existence, such as the following: (i) traditional operators have had time to optimize production processes and achieve lower costs, giving them an efficiency advantage over potential new entrants, (ii) companies in the market were able to produce large quantities, allowing them to benefit from economies of scale, and (iii) companies had time to introduce their products, and thus enjoy a reputation effect.

On the other hand, the higher the installation costs, the less entry there will be. Furthermore, these also constitute exit costs and correspond to sunk costs.

Concentration and Fixed Costs

In many cases, the presence of fixed costs explains why the average total cost decreases as output increases. This factor explains the existence of economies of scale—whereby higher production levels lead to lower average total costs for the firm. As a result of this dynamic, larger firms can sell at lower prices than smaller competitors, often leading to high market concentration or even corporate monopolies. New entrants typically begin with lower production volumes, putting them at a cost disadvantage compared to established firms. This cost gap effectively acts as a barrier to entry.

Stiglitz (1987) shows that, in a market with homogeneous products, the existence of sunk costs (even minimal ones) is sufficient to serve as a barrier to entry.

In this context, we can distinguish three types of barriers: natural barriers, artificial barriers, and strategic barriers.

Natural Barriers Inherent to the mechanisms of competition. For instance, in certain industries, learning time is required (advanced techniques), or there are economies of scale. Consequently, the potential entrant will have to invest heavily in research and production learning to compete. Consequently, the potential entrant will have to invest heavily in research and production learning to be able to compete.

Artificial Barriers Companies already established can prevent others from entering through a large number of brands (aimed at different types of customers), high spending on advertising, patents and licenses, control of suppliers (exclusivity contracts), etc., thereby discouraging the entry of potential competitors.

Strategic Barriers To concentrate market power, firms can carry out strategic actions focused on preventing the entry of other companies, including decisions on location, development and innovation, vertical integration, etc.

Barriers to entry are key to explaining the behavior and performance of companies. In the absence of barriers to entry and exit, the market is considered a contestable market.

Theory of Contestable Markets
According to the theory of contestable markets (Baumol et al. 1982), the number of firms in a market is not an indicator of the degree of competition in that market.

The market price may correspond to the price of perfect competition, even if there is only one firm in this market. The reason is the following: suppose there is a monopolistic firm in the market, but other firms can enter. If the incumbent firm sets a price above the perfectly competitive level—where firms earn zero economic profit—potential entrants will be incentivized to enter the market by offering a lower price. This competition drives the incumbent's profit down to zero economic profit. Consequently, the incumbent is forced to set a price equal to the perfectly competitive level to deter entry and maintain its market position.

Therefore, in a contestable market, firms lack market power and are limited by competition, even if it is a monopoly.

The theory of contestable markets legitimized some market deregulation decisions in the 1980s. Although this theory is valid, governments do not intervene to prevent a firm from becoming a monopoly or to regulate monopolistic behavior.

Therefore, the role of government is to ensure that markets are open to the entry of new firms since the presence of barriers to entry or exit increases the market power of established firms. Several authors have questioned the validity of the theory of contestable markets due to its very specific assumptions (including the possibility for potential participants to enter and exit the market instantly and at no cost).

6.5 To Remember

Competition policy promotes the creation of an environment conducive to business development and industrial cooperation (research and development).

The origin of competition policy is the United States in the nineteenth century with the appearance of the *trusts*.

Competition policy in the European Union aims to ensure fair competition between companies, which provides consumers with a variety of choices and lower prices for good quality products, through innovation.
Market power is the ability of a firm to increase its price above its marginal cost (perfect competition price).
Defining concentration is necessary for the following reasons: (i) determine to what extent a market is concentrated, and (ii) compare the market in question with others from the perspective of concentration.

6.6 Suggested Questions

1. In a principal-agent problem, the principal is the individual who ...... and hires the services of an agent to make decisions that will directly affect ....

    a. Has less information, the welfare of the principal.
    b. Has moral risk and adverse credit selection.
    c. Produces a public good, the welfare of society.
    d. Generates an externality, the wealth of the agent.

2. The adverse selection problem deals with a problem of:

    a. Information symmetry, whose solution is a separating contract.
    b. Information asymmetry, whose solution is a preparatory contract.
    c. Information symmetry, which has no solution.
    d. Information asymmetry, whose solution is a separating contract.

3. The instruments of competition policy regarding the abuse of the dominant position are:

    a. Article 82 ECT, Sherman Act Section 2, Clayton Act Section 3.
    b. Article 82 ECT, Sherman Act Section 2, Clayton Act Section 2.
    c. Article 81 ECT, Sherman Act Section 2, Clayton Act Section 3.
    d. None of the above

4. The correlation of prices over time is an element of:

    a. Set of prices.
    b. Set of principles.
    c. Set of indicia.
    d. set of choices.

5. Competition policy seeks primarily to:
    a. Ensure that monopolies maximize their profits.
    b. Protect consumer welfare and market efficiency.
    c. Favor the formation of oligopolies in strategic sectors.
    d. Prevent the development of multinational companies.
6. The concept of barriers to entry includes:
    a. Factors that facilitate the entry of new companies into the market.
    b. Legal, economic, or technical obstacles that hinder the entry of new competitors.
    c. Government regulations that reduce market power.
    d. None of the above.
7. Market concentration analysis uses tools such as:
    a. The Gini Index.
    b. The Herfindahl-Hirschman Index (HHI).
    c. The correlation coefficient.
    d. The Lorenz curve.
8. A practice considered anticompetitive under competition policy is:
    a. The setting of minimum prices among competitors.
    b. The free determination of prices by companies.
    c. The entry of new competitors into the market.
    d. The creation of economies of scale.
9. Abuse of dominant position occurs when:
    a. A firm uses its market position to limit competition.
    b. A firm maximizes its operating efficiency.
    c. Several firms compete on equal terms.
    d. Barriers to entry are eliminated.
10. The solution to the moral hazard problem in contract theory includes:
    a. The use of linear and flexible contracts.
    b. Incentives designed to align the interests of the agent and the principal.
    c. Complete elimination of the agent in the decisions of the principal.
    d. The standardization of all contracts.

CHAPTER 7

Answer Exercises

7.1 Answers to the Questions Suggested in Chap. 1

Choose the correct answer.

1. In a market economy, prices
   a. Are coordinated by the decisions of consumers and firms.
2. Under perfect competition, which of the following conditions would result in the short-run marginal cost curve not correctly reflecting the supply behavior of a profit-maximizing firm?
   b. Price exceeds average total cost.
3. If price equals short-run average variable cost, the firm is at the point known as the
   c. Shutdown point.
4. In a market economy, the price of a good
   b. Is set in the market.

C. Lanchimba, *Industrial Organization*,
https://doi.org/10.1007/978-3-032-10906-4_7

5. The supply and demand curve

    b. Synthesizes optimal production and consumption decisions, respectively

6. Demand curves shift because

    a. Revenues change.

7. A perfectly competitive industry will be in long-run equilibrium

    b. If there are no incentives for profit-maximizing firms to enter or exit the industry.

8. In a short-run competitive market, 60 firms operate, each with a cost function given by $CT = 12 + q^2$. The firm's supply curve is

    c. $P = 6q$.

9. One night, Toribio decides to eat cannelloni (c) and *a* chocolate bar (b), according to the function $U(c, b) = 20\ ln(c) + 18\ ln(b)$. How many cannelloni and chocolate bars does he consume that night? (Cost is not a factor.) However, doctors have recently recommended that Toribio limit his consumption of cannelloni and chocolate to 5. How many cannelloni and chocolate bars will he consume under these new circumstances?

    He consumes an infinite number of cannelloni and chocolate bars because his utility increases as the number of units increases, without restrictions. Therefore, under the new circumstances, he consumes 2.63 cannelloni and 2.37 chocolate bars.

10. A perfectly competitive industry has a large number of potential entrants. Each firm has the same cost structure, so the long-run average cost is minimized at a production level of 20 units ($q_i = 20$). The minimum average cost is \$10 per unit. Total market demand is given by $Q = 1500 - 50P$. What is the long-run equilibrium price (P^*), total industry output (Q^*), and number of firms?

    $P^* = 10$, $Q = 1000$ total output, $n = 50$ firms, and $\pi = 0$ in the long run

7.2 Answers to the Questions Suggested in Chap. 2

1. Suppose that Mr. Camilo Lopez is the only producer of televisions: Is he guaranteed to always make a profit?

   a. Monopolies do not always make a profit.
   Monopolies do not always make a profit. Losses can occur if costs are too high or demand is too low.

2. Which of the following is a characteristic of a monopoly?

   d. A single firm in the market.

3. Which of the following can create a monopoly?

   I. High prices.
   II. Patent.
   III. Government license.
   IV. Exclusive distribution of a good.
   d. II, III, and IV.

4. Compared to a competitive market, a monopoly:

   c. Reduces the quantity supplied and raises prices.

5. Select the type of market in which all firms sell identical products; neither buyers nor sellers can influence the price.

   a. Perfect competition.

6. Which of the following statements is true at the optimal output level for a monopoly?

   b. Price is greater than marginal cost.

7. A firm's marginal cost is defined as

   c. The additional cost of producing one more unit of output.

8. Price discrimination refers to the ability to

   a. Sell identical products at different prices.

9. Suppose an industry in perfect competition produces candles at a constant marginal cost of $10 per unit. Marginal costs when monopoly is established increase to $12 per unit because $2 must be paid to

other groups to maintain the monopoly position. Suppose the market demand for these candles is determined by $Q^D = 1000 - 50P$.

a. Calculate the output level and prices under perfect competition.
   $Q = 500$ and $P = 10$.
b. Calculate the output level and prices under monopolization.
   $Q = 200$ and $P = 16$
c. Calculate the total loss in consumer surplus under monopolization of appliance production.

   Under perfect competition = 2500
   Under monopoly = 400
   Total loss = 2100
   Deadweight loss = 900

d. Calculate the deadweight loss in efficiency (use a graph).
   Figure 7.1

10. A monopolist has to decide how to allocate its output between two geographically separated markets. The demand and marginal revenue for the two markets are $P_1 = 15 - Q_1$; $IMg_1 = 15 - 2Q_1$ and $P_2 = 25 - 2Q_2$; $IMg_2 = 25 - 4Q_2$. The monopolist's total cost is $C = 5 + 3(Q_1 + Q_2)$. Determine the market price, the level of production and the profits, if:

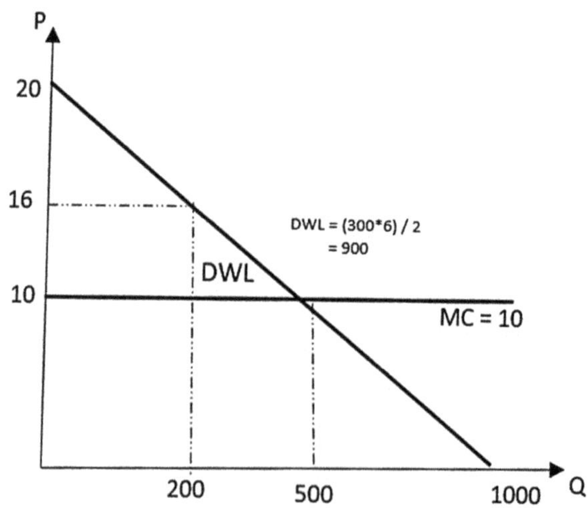

Fig. 7.1 Calculation of deadweight loss. Source: Author

a. It is a pure monopolist.
   $Q = 11.5$, $P = 10.67$, and $\pi = 83.1$
b. The monopolist can practice price discrimination by splitting markets.
   $Q_1 = 6, P_1 = 9$; $Q_2 = 5.5$; $P_2 = 14$, and $\pi = 91.50$

7.3 Answers to the Questions Suggested in Chap. 3

1. A typical monopolistically competitive market is for

   d. Home appliances.

2. In monopolistic competition, there are

   a. Many firms making a differentiated product.

3. Dole Co. operates in a monopolistically competitive market. Which of the following characterizes Dole Co.'s market?

   d. All of the above describe Dole Co.'s market.

4. Which of the following is NOT a characteristic of monopolistic competition?

   b. Price-taking firms.

5. The key characteristic of monopolistic competition that distinguishes it from perfect competition is

   d. Product differentiation.

6. Perfect competition and monopolistic competition are similar in that both market structures include

   c. No barriers to entry.

7. Each firm's demand curve in monopolistic competition has

   b. Negative slope, and there are no barriers to entry into the market.

8. Monopoly and monopolistic competition are different because

   b. There are no barriers to entry in monopolistic competition.

9. In monopolistic competition,

   b. Firms have market power, the ability to sell beyond marginal cost.

10. Suppose that firms compete by selling differentiated products but not perfect substitutes. Additionally, there is free entry and exit of firms. What market structure best describes the previous situation?

    c. Monopolistic competition

7.4 Answers to the Questions Suggested in Chap. 4

1. In a duopoly, Cournot equilibrium occurs when both companies

    c. Have the ability to simultaneously affect the price of the good.

2. In a duopoly, Edgeworth equilibrium occurs when both companies

    b. Have production limitations.

3. Bertrand's paradox means that

    c. Both companies have zero profits.

4. When analyzing a market, it is observed that the equilibrium quantity and price coincide for a prolonged period of time with the quantity and price that correspond to the monopoly, but in said market, several companies operate, from the supply. It can be said that it is

    c. A cartel.

5. The oligopoly differs from monopolistic competition because in the oligopoly

    b. There are barriers to entry.

6. Among the models exclusively of price competition are

    a. Bertrand model and Edgeworth model.

7. In a cartel, the group of firms seeks to

    b. Maximize joint profit.

8. The Stackelberg model is more appropriate than the Cournot model in situations where

    c. One firm makes its production decision before the other.

9. When firms are symmetric, that is, they have the same costs, then

   a. The Stackelberg solution is more efficient than the Cournot solution (higher total quantity, lower price).

10. The inverse demand curve for the bicycle market is given by $P = 100 - Q$, where $Q = q1 + q2$, and the cost of each firm is given by $C(q_i) = 20q_i + \frac{q_i^2}{2}$, $i = 1.2$.

    a. Determine the reaction curves.
       $q_1 = \frac{80}{3} - \frac{q_2}{3}; q_2 = \frac{80}{3} - \frac{q_1}{3}$
    b. Determine the Cournot equilibrium.
       $Q = 40; P = 60; \pi_1 = 600 = \pi_2$
    c. Determine the Stackelberg equilibrium.
       $Q = 42; P = 58; \pi_1 = 610; \pi_2 = 544$

7.5 Answers to the Questions Suggested in Chap. 5

1. An example of moral hazard is

   d. All of the above.

2. What is adverse selection?

   b. A process where parties with asymmetric information select the least desirable outcomes.

3. What is a signal in information economics?

   b. An action that reveals credible information to the other party.

4. What is an incentive mechanism?

   b. A system that aligns the interests of the parties involved through rewards or punishments.

5. What is uncertainty in economics?

   b. The lack of certainty about future outcomes.

6. What is risk in economic terms?

   a. The probability of a negative event occurring.

7. What is insurance in economics?

    b. A contract to transfer risk from one party to another.

8. What is diversification in investment terms?

    b. The spreading of investments across several assets to reduce risk.

9. What does risk aversion represent?

    a. The preference to avoid uncertainty and risk.

10. What is moral hazard?

    b. Different behavior by a person when protected from consequences.

7.6 Answers to the Questions Suggested in Chap. 6

1. In a principal-agent problem, the principal is the individual who ...... and hires the services of an agent to make decisions that will directly affect ......

    a. Has less information, the welfare of the principal.

2. The adverse selection problem deals with a problem of

    d. Information asymmetry, whose solution is a separating contract.

3. The instruments of competition policy regarding the abuse of the dominant position are

    b. Article 82 of the ECT, Sherman Act Section 2, Clayton Act Section 2.

4. The correlation of prices over time is an element of

    c. Set of signals.

5. Competition policy mainly seeks to

    b. Protect consumer welfare and market efficiency.

6. The concept of entry barriers includes

b. Legal, economic, or technical obstacles that hinder the entry of new competitors.

7. Market concentration analysis uses tools such as

   b. The Herfindahl-Hirschman index (HHI).

8. A practice considered anticompetitive under competition policy is

   a. Setting minimum prices among competitors.

9. Abuse of a dominant position occurs when

   a. A firm uses its position in the market to limit competition.

10. The solution to the moral hazard problem in contract theory includes

    b. Incentives designed to align the interests of the agent and the principal.

CHAPTER 8

Appendix

8.1 Appendix 1: Game Theory

Game theory is a tool for studying strategic problems. A game in the strict sense is any situation where economic agents (players) must choose strategies, cooperating with other agents or not (strategies) to achieve a desired result (payoff). Players, strategies, and payoff are the basic elements of the game.

Nash Equilibrium is similar to Pareto equilibrium, i.e., no one wants to change their behavior.

If a player X chooses x^* as an optimal strategy (this represents their best strategy) instead of y^* and Y chooses y^* instead of x^*, (x^*, y^*) represent a Nash equilibrium solution. This can be represented as

$$U_X(x^*, y^*) \geq U_X(x', y^*) \vee x' \subset E_X \text{ y } U_Y(x^*, y^*) \geq U_X(x^*, y') \vee y' \subset E_Y$$

where U_X, U_Y is the utility of players X and Y, respectively, provided by the strategy they chose and E_X, E_Y is the set of possible strategies for each player.

Observations

– A game can have multiple equilibria.

C. Lanchimba, *Industrial Organization*,
https://doi.org/10.1007/978-3-032-10906-4_8

Table 8.1 Example payoff. Source: Author

	Mountain	Beach
Mountain	(2,1)	(0,0)
Beach	(0,0)	(1,2)

Table 8.2 Example of mobile telephony. Source: Author

		Movistar	
		Weak	Strong
Clear	Weak	(1.1)	(2.0)
	Strong	(0.2)	(4.4)

– Some equilibria may be undesirable.

An example might be when a couple has to decide between getting married on the beach or in the mountains, assuming that the game provides the following payoffs (Table 8.1):

In this case, it can be observed that there is no equilibrium, so the solution would be to include a strategy with probabilities that in this case would be represented by flipping a coin (mixed strategy.)

Example: Claro and Movistar Ecuador Mobile telephony is one of the sectors with the highest profits in Ecuador, with a market penetration of 99.6% (Metrics, 2024). The mobile operators Claro (América Móvil), Movistar (Telefónica), and CNT (Estado del Ecuador) control 100% of the Ecuadorian market (Telesemana, 2023).

In this context, no operator communicates its marketing plan for mobile devices such as the iPhone. However, both companies often make very tempting offers to their users in order to attract customers. So, knowing that both companies control the mobile market, what should their marketing investment be?

Table 8.2 represents fictitious values of the strategies, taking into account those of the competition. In this case, the best strategy is to make a high investment in marketing. Indeed, this is what can be observed in the Ecuadorian reality, where if one of the companies launches a promotion, the other will do so immediately. Therefore, a strong investment in marketing is observed by both companies.

8.2 Appendix 2: Empirical Evidence

Introduction of the papers by Brickley (1999) and Arruñada et al. (2001)

8.2.1 The Brickley (1999) Test

This article was published in the *The Journal of Law and Economics.*

Theoretical Fields

- Econometrics of franchise contracts
- Contract design
- Agency theory

Objective/Problem
Develop testable implications based on agency theory on three clauses commonly used in franchise contracts (complementary to the franchise restrictions):

i Restriction of the distributor's external activities
ii Territorial exclusivity
iii Participation in the network's promotion effort

It tries to show that the forms of organization vary systematically with the level of external factors.

Method
Development of a theoretical model that highlights the conditions that encourage franchisees to underinvest in the promotion effort. In this context, three situations are distinguished depending on the level of horizontal externalities:

i Franchise contract without vertical restrictions when externalities are low
ii Franchise contract associated with vertical restrictions with an intermediate degree of externalities
iii The retail unit linked to the wholesaler with a high degree of externalities

The qualitative predictions derived from this model are subject to econometric tests, from a sample of companies belonging to large franchise chains through three binary logit models (one model per vertical restriction).

Predictions Tested

H1 Vertical restrictions associated with franchise contracts increase with the level of externalities between units in the same chain.
H2 Chains within which the wholesaler owns a significant proportion of the retail units tend to include vertical restrictions in their franchise contracts.

Result, Conclusions, and Limits

R1 Validation of H1.
R2 Most of the tests do not validate H2.
R3 The correlation matrix of the dependent variables shows that these clauses are complementary. Referring to Holmstrom and Milgrom (1994) on complementary clauses, the contract is a system of complementary clauses.

8.2.2 The Arrunada, Garnicano, Vazquez Test (2001)

This article was published in the *Journal of Law, Economics, and Organization.*

Theoretical Fields

- Econometrics of franchise agreements
- Contract design
- Agency theory

Objective/Problem

Empirical study of contractual solutions to moral hazard problems in franchise relationships. Moral hazard is at the heart of the explanation.

Vertical and horizontal externalities are caused by the risk of opportunistic behavior on both sides, franchisor and franchisee (double moral hazard).

The objective is to study the impact of moral hazard on the distribution of powers in decision-making between franchisor and franchisee.

Method

A sectoral study is carried out (franchise contracts in the automobile sector). The authors have direct access to the contracts of 23 networks. Contracts are standardized by network, distinguishing three categories of clauses, i.e., rights granted to the industrialist: (i) ex post complementary rights, (ii) control rights, and (iii) rights to break the contract.

The dependent variable is an index constructed by aggregating the number of rights given to the industrialist in each area (complement, control, break). The three explanatory variables used are the average price of the car brand, the number of retailers in the network, and the age of the network.

The estimation is carried out with the help of the ordinary least squares method by category of rights. Finally, they carry out an extension to study the complementarities between the clauses from a correlation matrix between the endogenous variables.

Predictions Tested

- H1 The opportunism of distributors increases with the quality of the products (cars); quality is the market segment. H0 according to which moral hazard (unobservable sales effort) is more important when quality is high.
- H2 As for any public good, the larger the network (number of retailers), the higher the horizontal externality. Therefore, a positive correlation is expected between the size of the network and the decision-making and control powers of the industrialist.
- H3 Reputation (age of the network), a correlation like the previous one is expected.

Results, Conclusions, and Limits

Despite the small size of the sample, the results are interesting and systematically confirm the theoretical explanation.

- R1 All contracts severely limit the decision-making powers of franchisees.
- R2 Confirmation of H0 according to which moral hazard is a source of variation in contractual terms, i.e., the role of moral hazard in the structure of contracts.
- R3 The results are very interesting, since a correlation between the clauses is evident, highlighting the complementarity between various categories of clauses.

References

Ackerlof, G. 1970. The market for lemons: Quality uncertainty and the market mechanism. *Journal of Law Economics and Organization*, 84 (3): 488–500.

Apple Inc. 2007. At&t y apple anuncian planes de servicio simples y asequibles para iphone. https://www.apple.com/newsroom/2007/06/26AT-T-and-Apple-Announce-Simple-Affordable-Service-Plans-for-iPhone/. Access on December 2024.

Apple Inc. 2024. Información jurídica: Propiedad intelectual. https://www.apple.com/es/legal/intellectual-property/. Access on December 2024.

Arrow, J., and G. Debreu. 1954. Existence of an equilibrium for a competitive economy. *Econometrica* 22: 265–290.

Arruñada, Benito, L. Garnicano, and L. Vázquez. 2001. Contractual allocation of decision rights and incentives: The case of automobile distribution. *Journal of Law Economics and Organization* 7: 257–286.

Atanasof, D. 2024. Tendencias recientes en la participación global de Windows en el mercado. https://perspectivainternacional.com/tendencias-recientes-en-la-participacion-global-de-windows-en-el-mercado/. Access on June 2024.

Bain, J. 1956. *Barriers to New Competition*. Cambridge: Harvard University Press.

Bain, J. 1959. *Industrial Organization: A Treatise*. London: Wiley.

Baker, G. 1960. An economic analysis of fertility. In *Demographic and Economic Change in Developed Countries*. New York: Columbia University Press.

Balan, David, Patrick DeGraba, Francine Lafontaine, Patrick McAlvanah, and Devesh Raval. 2015. Economics at the FTC: Fraud, mergers and exclusion. *Review of Industrial Organization* 47: 371–398.

C. Lanchimba, *Industrial Organization*,
https://doi.org/10.1007/978-3-032-10906-4

Baumol, William, John Panzar, and Robert Willig. 1982. *Contestable Markets and the Theory of Industry Structure*. New York: Harcourt Brace Jovanovich.
BBC News. 2014. Facebook to buy messaging app WhatsApp for $19bn. https://www.bbc.com/news/business-26266689. Access on December 2024.
Blair, R., and F. Lafontaine. 2005. *The Economics of Franchising*, 1st ed. Cambridge: Cambridge University Press.
Bloomberg. 2018. Quiebras: Guerra con Amazon deja cada vez más víctimas entre supermercados. https://www.df.cl/empresas/retail/quiebras-guerra-con-amazon-deja-cada-vez-mas-victimas-entre-supermercados. Access on December 2024.
Boiteux, M. 1956. Sur la gestion des monopoles publics astrient á l equilibre budgetaire. *Econometrica* 24: 22–40.
Bolton, P., and M. Dewatripont. 2005. *Contract Theory*. Cambridge: The MIT Press.
Brickley, J. A. 1999. Incentive conflicts and contractual restraints: Evidence from franchising. *Journal of Law and Economics* 42: 745–774.
Brickley, J. A., and F. H. Dark. 1987. The choice of organizational form: The case of franchising. *Journal of Financial Economics* 18: 401–420.
Brito-Rhor, M., and J. Borja. 2015. Estrategias de Pepsi. https://mktadstrategies.wordpress.com/2016/03/24/5-estrategias-de-pepsi/. Access on December 2024.
Cain, A. 2022. The history of amazon and whole foods' sometimes-rocky marriage, which kicked off 5 years ago with a $13.7 billion acquisition. https://www.businessinsider.com/amazon-whole-foods-market-history-2022-8. Access on December 2024.
Carlton, D., and M. Perloff. 2008. *Economie Industrielle*. Edition DeBoeck.
CentroCompetencia (CeCo). 2021. La industria automotriz alemana y el primer caso de colusión en los estándares ambientales. https://centrocompetencia.com/la-industria-automotriz-alemana-y-el-primer-caso-de-colusion-en-los-estandares-ambientales/. Access on December 2024.
Chai, L., D. Wu, A. Dolgui, and Y. Duan. 2020. Pricing strategy for b&m store in a dual-channel supply chain based on hotelling model. *International Journal of Production* 59 (18): 5578–5591.
Chamberlin, Edward. 1933. *The Theory of Monopolistic Competition*. Cambridge, Mass: Harvard University Press.
Coase, R. H. 1937. *The Nature of the Firm, in: The Firm, the Market, and the Law*. Chicago: University of Chicago Press.
Comanor, William, and Patrick Rey. 1997. Competition policy towards vertical restraints in Europe and the United States. *Empirica* 24 (1): 37–52.
Comisión Europea. 2014. Comprender las políticas de la Compentencia en la Unión Europea. http://publications.europa.eu/resource/cellar/9f857b2ee25a-4fc3-9550-81a9de3b0429.0008.02/DOC_1. Access on June 2016.

Comisión Europea. 2019a Definición de mercado de referencia. https://eur-lex.europa.eu/legal-content/ES/TXT/?uri=LEGISSUM%3Al26073. Access on June 2019.

Comisión Europea. 2019b Las instituciones de la UE y la política de competencia. http://ec.europa.eu/competition/consumers/institutions_es.html. Access on June 2019.

Comisión Europea. 2021. Antitrust: Commission fines car manufacturers €875 million for restricting competition in emission cleaning for new diesel passenger cars. https://ec.europa.eu/commission/presscorner/detail/ro/ip_21_3581. Access on December 2024.

Congressional Research Service. 2018. Gas exporting countries forum (GECF): Cartel lite? https://crsreports.congress.gov/product/pdf/IF/IF10939. Access on December 2024.

Cornestone Research. 2019. United states v. at&t inc. et al. https://www.cornerstone.com/insights/cases/united-states-v-att/. Access on December 2024.

Corte Suprema Comisión Europea. 2021. Judgment of the general court (ninth chamber, extended composition). https://constitutioncenter.org/news-debate. https://eur-lex.europa.eu/legal-content/EN/TXT/?uri=celex%3A62017TJ0612. Access on December 2024.

Corte Suprema di cassazione. 2019. Sentenza cassazione civile. https://www.avvocato.it/massimario-12201/. Access on December 2024.

Cournot, A. 1838. *Recherches sur les principes mathématiques de la théorie des richesses.* Paris: Hachette.

Court of Justice of the European Union. 2024. Judgment of the Court of Justice (Grand Chamber) of 10 September 2024. European Commission v Ireland and Apple Sales International (Case C-465/20 P)

Demsetz, H. 1968. Toward a theory of property rights. *American Economic Review* 57: 347–359.

DOJ. 2019. United states v. at and t, inc., no. 18-5214. https://law.justia.com/cases/federal/appellate-courts/cadc/18-5214/18-5214-2019-02-26.html. Access on December 2024.

Dorfman, R., and P. Steiner. Optimal advertising and optimal quality. *American Economic Review* 44: 826–836.

Estudio, Elio 2024. La historia de "just do it", la estrategia de branding que marcó un legado. https://elioestudio.com/la-historia-de-just-do-it/. Access on December 2024.

Friedman, A., and S. Miles. 2002. Developing stakeholder theory. *Journal of Management Studies* 39 (1): 1–21.

General Motors. 2023 La planta de GM OBB del ecuador entre las más destacadas de los manufacturing awards 2023 de General Motors. https://media.gm.

com/media/ec/es/chevrolet/home.detail.html/content/Pages/news/ec/es/2023/dec/1220-produccione.html. Access on December 2024.

Global de Marketing de Grupo Bimbo. 2024. Bimbo es la marca de alimentos más elegida por los hogares en México y Latinoamérica. https://www.grupobimbo.com/es/prensa/comunicados/liderazgo/bimbo-es-la-marca-de-alimentos-mas-elegida-por-los-hogares-en-mexico-y. Access on December 2024.

Green, Edward, and Robert Porter. 1984. Noncooperative collusion under imperfect price information. *Econometrica* 52 (1): 87–100.

Harris, M., and A. Raviv. 1979. Optimal incentive contracts with imperfect information. *Journal Economic Theory* 20: 231–259.

Hart, O., and B. Holmstrom. 1987. The theory of contract. In *Advances in Economic theory, Fifth World Congress.* Cambridge: Cambridge University Press.

Holmstrom, B. 1979. Moral hazard and observability. *Bell Journal of Economics* 10 (1): 74–91.

Hotelling, H. 1929. Stability in competition. *The Economic Journal* 39 (153): 41–57.

Kaufmann, P., and R. Dant. 1996. Multi-unit franchising: growth and management issues. *Journal of Business Venturing* 11 (5): 343–358.

Kay, J. 1990. Vertical restraints in European competition policy. *European Economic Review* 34 (2–3): 551–561.

Kisswani, M. 2011. Does OPEC act as a cartel? empirical investigation of coordination behavior. *Energy Policy* 97: 171–180.

Krueger. 1991. Ownership, agency and wages: An examination of franchising in the fast food industry. *Quarterly Journal of Economics* 106: 75–101.

Kumar, R. 2019. *Procter & Gamble's Acquisition of Gillette.* Berlin: Springer.

Laffont, J. 2006. Á propos de l'é mergence de la thé orie des incitations. *Revue francaise de gestion* 160: 177–189.

Laffont, J. J., and D. Martimort. 2001. *The Theory of Incentives: The Principal-Agent Model.* Princeton: Princeton University Press.

Lafontaine, F. 1992a. Agency theory and franchising some empirical results. *RAND Journal of Economics* 23: 263–283.

Lafontaine, F. 1992b. How and why do franchisors do what they do: A survey report. In *Sixth Annual Proceedings of the Society of Franchising.*

Lafontaine, F., and P. Kaufmann. 1994. The evolution of ownership patterns in franchise systems. *Journal of Retailing* 70 (2): 97–113.

Lafontaine, F., and E. Raynaud. 2000. Créance résiduelle et flux de rentes comme mécanismes incitatifs dans les contrats de franchise : compléments ou substituts? *Revue d'Economie Industrielle* 92: 255–276.

Lancaster, Kelvin 1966. A new approach to consumer theory. *Journal of Political Economy* 74 (2): 132–157.

Lancaster, Kelvin. 1971. *Consumer Demand: A New Approach.* New York: Columbia University Press.

Lancaster, Kelvin. 1979. *Variety, Equity and Efficiency.* New York: Columbia University Press.

Lanchimba, C., and D. Diaz. 2017. Efectos de los ingresos del hogar, educación de la mujer y participación laboral femenina sobre la fecundidad ecuatoriana. *Economic Analysis Review* 32 (1): 47–67.

Lee, E. 2020. T-mobile closes merger with sprint, and a wireless giant is born. https://www.nytimes.com/2020/04/01/business/media/tmobile-closes-sprint-merger.html. Access on December 2024.

Liebowitz, S., and S. Margolis. 2001. *Winners, Losers and Microsoft Competition and Antitrust in High Technology.* Independent Institute.

LSA Magazine. 2008. Neptune et cristaline changent de mains. https://www.lsa-conso.fr/neptune-et-cristaline-changent-de-mains,66633. Access on December 2024.

Mas-Colell, A., M. Whinston, and J. Green. 1995. *Microeconomic Theory.* Oxford: Oxford University Press.

Mason, E. 1939. Price and production policies of large-scale enterprise. *American Economic Review* 29 (1): 61–74.

Mathewson, F., and R. Winter. 1984. An economic theory of vertical restraints. *RAND Journal of Economics* 15: 27–38.

Mathewson, F., and R. Winter. 1985. The economics of franchise contracts. *Journal of Law and Economics* 28: 503–526.

Medan, P., and T. Warin. 2000. *Economie industrielle: Une perspective européenne*, 1st ed. Dunod.

Metrics, Digital. 2024. 61% de las líneas móviles en ecuador son lte. http://dplnews.com/61-de-las-lineas-moviles-en-ecuador-son-lte/. Access on December 2024.

Milgrom, P., and J. Roberts. 1992. *Economics, Organization and Management. Prentice-Hall International*, 1st ed.. Saddle River: Prentice-Hall International.

Minkler, A. P. 1990. An empirical analysis of a firm's decision to franchise. *Economics Letters* 34: 77–82.

Moreno, Natalia. 2021. Google vs commission (google shopping): A case summary. *SSRN Electronic Journal* 1–6. https://doi.org/10.2139/ssrn.3965639

Motta, M. 2006. *Competition Policy: Theory and Practice.* Cambridge: Cambridge University Press.

Movistar. 2024. Ofertas. https://www.movistar.com.ec/ofertas-movistar. Access on December 2024.

Nelson, P. 1970. Information and consumer behavior. *Journal of Political Economy* 78: 311–329.

Nelson, P. 1974. Advertising as information. *Journal of Political Economy* 82: 729–754.

Nelson, P. 1978. Advertising as information once more. In *Issues in Advertising: The Economics of Persuasion*, 133–160. Washington, D. C.: American Enterprise Institute for Public Policy Research.

Norton, S. 1988. An empirical look at franchising as an organizational form. *Journal of Business* 61: 197–217.

Orús, A. 2024. Consumo per cápita de bebidas refrescantes a nivel mundial en 2023. https://es.statista.com/previsiones/1292261/ventas-per-capita-en-el-mercado-de-refrescos-a-nivel-mundial-por-pais. Access on December 2024.

Organisation for Economic Co-operation and Development (OECD). 2000. Hard Core Cartels. *OECD Journal of Competition Law and Policy*, 2 (2).

Organización para la Cooperación y el Desarrollo Económicos (OCDE). 2007. Derecho y política de la competencia en América Latina. http://www.fne.gob.cl/wp-content/uploads/2017/10/oecd_0001_2007.pdf. Access on June 2019.

Pancras, J., S. Sriram, and V. Kumar. 2012. Empirical investigation of retail expansion and cannibalization in a dynamic environment. *Management Science* 58 (11): 2001–2012.

Pénard, T., E. Raynaud, and S. Saussier. 2004. Monitoring policy and organizational forms in franchised chains. *Revue Française d'Économie* 18: 151–191.

Perloff, J. M. 2007. *Microeconomics (4th ed.)*. Pearson Education, Inc.

Pettinger, T. 2020. Collusion - meaning. https://www.economicshelp.org/blog/21475/economics/collusion-meaning-and-examples/. Access on December 2024.

Pfister, Etienne, Bruno Deffains, Myriam Doriat-Duban, and Stéphane Saussier. 2006. Institutions and contracts: Franchising. *European Journal of Law and Economics* 21 (1): 53–78.

Pindyck, R., and S. Rubinfeld. 2009. *Microeconomía*. Upper Saddle River: Pearson Prentice Hall.

Posada, Camilo. 2019. Concentraciones empresariales: el caso siemens/alstom. https://www.ambitojuridico.com/noticias/especiales/concentraciones-empresariales-el-caso-siemensalstom. Access on December 2024.

Posner, Richard. 1975. The social costs of monopoly and regulation. *Journal of Political Economy* 4: 807–828.

Ray, Siladitya. 2024. Apple must pay $14.3 billion in back taxes, top eu court rules. https://www.forbes.com/sites/siladityaray/2024/09/10/apple-must-pay-143-billion-in-back-taxes-top-eu-court-rules/. Access on December 2024.

Reault, Groupe, 2016. Un groupe fort de son alliance unique. https://group.renault.com/groupe/un-groupe-une-alliance-des-partenariats/un-groupe-fort-de-son-alliance-unique

República del Ecuador. 2011. Organic Law for the Regulation and Control of Market Power (Ley Orgánica de Regulación y Control del Poder de Mercado). Official Register Supplement No. 555, Quito, Ecuador.

Rey, P., and F. Caballero-Sanz. 1996. The policy implications of economic analysis of vertical restraints. *Economic Papers European Commissio*, 19.

Rey, P., and J. Tirole. 1986. The logic of vertical restraints. *American Economic Review* 76 (5): 921–939.

Ridder, M. 2024. Leading carbonated soft drink (CSD) companies in the united states in 2022. https://www.statista.com/statistics/225504/leading-carbonated-soft-drink-companies-in-the-us/#statisticContainer. Access on December 2024.

Robinson, Joan. 1934. What is perfect competition? *The Quarterly Journal of Economic* 49 (1): 104–120.

Rosen, Jeffrey. 2020. United states v. google. Podcast en: https://constitutioncenter.org/news-debate/podcasts/united-states-v-google?gad_source=1&gclid=EAIaIQobChMIxvT8vJqgigMVpIBaBR1GEwW8EAAYASAAEgJ–vD_BwE. Access on December 2024.

Salanié, Bernard. 2005. *The Economics of Contracts*. Cambridge: The MIT Press.

Samuelson, P., and W. Nordhaus. 2010. *Economía con aplicaciones a Latinoamérica*. Columbus: McGraw-Hill Interamericana.

Schumpeter, J. 1942. Capitalism, socialism and democracy. *Harper and Row* 36: 132–145.

Shapiro, C., and H. Varian. 2000. *El dominio de la información. Una guía estratégica para la economía de la red*. Antoni Bosh Edito.

Shepard, A. 1993. Contractual Form, Retail Price, and Asset Characteristics in Gasoline Retailing. *The RAND Journal of Economics 24* (1): 58–77. https://doi.org/10.2307/2555953.

Shepherd, W. 1984. Contestability vs. competition. *American Economic Review* 74 (4): 572–587.

Shuvanova, E., and E. Rohulia. 1942. The analysis of barriers to entry into the pharmaceutical market of Ukraine. *Research Journal of Pharmacy and Technology* 14 (12): 6353–6358.

Slade, M. E. 1996. Multitask Agency and Contract Choice: An Empirical Exploration. *International Economic Review 37* (2): 465–486.

Smith, Alex. 2021. Systembolaget: Sweden's state alcohol monopoly. https://drinks-intel.com/intel/interview/systembolaget-swedens-state-alcohol-monopoly/. Access on December 2024.

Soni, D. 2024. Incorporating "supply-side substitutability" in the definition of "relevant market". https://www.icle.in/resource/incorporating-supply-side-substitutability-in-the-definition-of-relevant-market-a-critical-analysis/. Access on December 2024.

Spence, A. M. 1973. Job market signaling. *Quarterly Journal of Economics* 87: 355–379.

Spengler, Joseph. 1950. Vertical integration and antitrust policy. *Journal of Political Economy* 58 (4): 347–352.

Statista. 2024. Amazon: Participación de mercado y estadísticas clave. https://es.statista.com/temas/3556/amazon/#topicOverview. Access on December 2024.

Stigler, G. 1971. The theory of economic regulation. *Bell Journal of Economics and Management Science* 2 (1): 120–135.

Stiglitz, Joseph. 1987. Pareto efficient and optimal taxation and the new new welfare economics. In *Handbook of Public Economics*, ed. A. J. Auerbach and M. Feldstein, vol. 2. Amsterdam: Elsevier.

Suki, N. 2013. Students' demand for smartphones: Structural relationships of product features, brand name, product price and social influence. *Campus-Wide Information Systems* 30 (4): 236–248.

Sutton, J. 1991. *Sunk Costs and Market Structure: Price Competition, Advertising, and the Evolution of Concentration*. Cambridge: MIT Press.

T-Mobile. 2020. T mobile lleva a cabo la fusión con Sprint para formar la nueva t mobile. https://es.t-mobile.com/news/un-carrier/t-mobile-sprint-one-company. Access on December 2024.

Taylor, J. 2002. The output effects of government sponsored cartels during the new deal. *Journal of Industrial Economics* 50 (1): 1–10.

Telesemana. 2023. Panorama de mercado – ecuador. www.telesemana.com/panorama-de-mercado/ecuador/. Access on December 2024.

Tirole, Jean. 1988. *The Theory of Industrial Organization*. Cambridge: The MIT Press.

Ultimate Specs. 2002. Comparación fiat grande punto 1.4 2006 frente a ford fiesta 6 1.4 2002 frente a ford fiesta 6 1.25i 2002. https://www.ultimatespecs.com/es/car-comparator/777,805,803/Fiat-Grande-Punto-vs-Ford-Fiesta-6-vs-Ford-Fiesta-6.html. Access on December 2024

Varian, H. 2015. *Microeconomía intermedia*. Antoni Bosh Editor.

Vázquez, L. 2004. Economics and management of franchising networks. In *The Use of Up-Front Fees, Royalties and Franchisor Sales to franchisees in Business Format Franchising*, ed. J. Windsperger, G. Cliquet, G. Hendrikse, M. Tuunanen, 145–159. Springer, Berlin.

Vickers, J., and G. Yarrow. 1988. *Privatization: An Economic Analysis*. Cambridge: MIT Press.

Williams, D. 1999. Why do entrepreneurs become franchisees? *Journal of Business Venturing* 14 (1): 103–124.

Yvrande-Billon, A., and S. Saussier. 2004. Do organization choices matter? Assessing the importance of governance through performance comparisons. In *New Ideas in Contracting and Organizational Economics Research*, ed. Harvey S. James. Dordrecht: Kluwer Academic Publishers.

Index

C. Lanchimba, *Industrial Organization*,
https://doi.org/10.1007/978-3-032-10906-4

GPSR Compliance
The European Union's (EU) General Product Safety Regulation (GPSR) is a set of rules that requires consumer products to be safe and our obligations to ensure this.

If you have any concerns about our products, you can contact us on

ProductSafety@springernature.com

In case Publisher is established outside the EU, the EU authorized representative is:

Springer Nature Customer Service Center GmbH
Europaplatz 3
69115 Heidelberg, Germany

www.ingramcontent.com/pod-product-compliance
Ingram Content Group UK Ltd.
Pitfield, Milton Keynes, MK11 3LW, UK
UKHW020827210626
472426UK00002B/44
* 9 7 8 3 0 3 2 1 0 9 0 5 7 *